HISTORICAL QUOTATIONS

*A Compilation of Quotations from
Recognized Authorities of Secular History,
Articulated with the Bible*

E. M. Zerr

Historical Quotations: A Compilation of Quotations from Recognized Authorities of Secular History, Articulated with the Bible

Copyright © 2024

Published by:
Gospel Armory Publishing
Bowling Green, Kentucky
www.GospelArmory.com

Printed in the United States of America

ISBN: 978-1-959201-40-3

PREFACE

This little volume is a gleaning from forty thousand pages of ancient history and other critical sources which I read through a period of twenty years. Early in my work as a teacher of the Bible I observed the value of such matter in explaining and confirming the prophetic and other technical statements of Holy Writ. In many instances even those writers classed as infidels were found to verify the divine declarations; not that they wished to write for this purpose, but, being conscientious historians, they gave historic matter that was corroborative of the very circumstances mentioned by the inspired writers.

But such vast amount of reading matter was not available to many readers of the Bible even if they had the time to examine it. And I realized that I could not have my histories at hand always, there being some thirty-one authors cited, and this led me to make quotations from these authors of the vital statements in point at given places in the Bible and to adopt a system of index signs (A—1, B—1, etc.) for reference to the several quotations and place these signs in my Bible at the various places where the historic quotation would be applicable. After using this work for some time, several readers of the Bible, seeing the advantage of such a condensed collection of these vital statements from history, suggested the idea of publishing them in convenient form for others who might not have the time or opportunity of such extensive reading, and yet who would desire the benefit of such information. For this reason this book is offered to you.

Where more than one author is given at the end of a quotation, the first one given is the one from whom the quotation is made and the others are cited as those who agree with the quotation. In the references to Josephus the sign, Ant. 12-7-6, mean Antiquities, Book 12, Chapter 7, Section 6. The signs mean the same as the numbers when Josephus' Wars is referred to. An index or key to various passages where these historic quotations may be applied will be found following the index. Of course, the Bible student will discover many additional places where they may be used as he pursues his studies.

That this little work may assist and encourage others in the study of the Sacred Text is the wish of the author.

E. M. ZERR
New Castle, Indiana

GENERAL INDEX

Mesopotamians carry their gods when they travel	1—A
Pools in Jerusalem	1—B
Origin of Gauls, Medes, and Greeks	1—C
Origin of the word Hebrew	1—D
Ishmael founder of the Arabians	1—E
The Ten Commandments	1—F
Daily sacrifice congregational	1—G
Date of first—fruits	1—H
Artaxerxes' treatment of the women	1—I
Many Jews carried into Egypt	1—J
Origin of the Septaugent	1—K
Circumcision disguised	1—L
An altar built in Egypt	1—M
One difference Pharisees and Sadusees	1—N
Period of Maccabees	1—O
Pompey takes Jerusalem; Herod succeeds Maccabees	1—P
Unlawful to kill out of Jerusalem	1—Q
Early Babylonian Empire	1—R
Rise of Assyrian Empire	1—S
Later Babylonian Empire	1—T
Origin and Kinship of Medes and Persians	1—U
Origin, Medo-Persian Empire; Medes at first in lead	1—V
Fall of Babylon	1—W
Macedonian Empire	1—X
Alexander's 'flying trip'	1—Y
None as strong as Alexander	1—Z
Alexander's Four Successors	2—A
The Roman Empire	2—B
Iron-like strength of Roman Empire	2—C
Greeks used arms of brass	2—D

"River of Egypt"	2—E
Josephus of the Priestly family	2—F
Meaning of the word Adam	2—G
Curse upon the serpent	2—H
Mid-wives were Egyptians	2—I
Arabians circumcise at 13th year	2—J
The Shepherd Kings	2—K
Date of Josephus' birth – his three sons	2—L
Offering of first-fruits	2—M
Espousal and marriage	2—N
Order in which the high priests served	2—O
Egyptians worshipped animals	2—P
Walls and gates of ancient Babylon	2—Q
Epiphanes stops daily sacrifice	2—R
His miraculous death	2—S
Cestius' Unaccountable Retreat	2—T
The Roman Eagle	2—U
The fig tree	2—V
Distress of siege of Jerusalem	2—W
Sedition of Jerusalem	2—X
Destruction of city of Babylon	2—Y
Feast of Bacchus	2—Z
The fall of Ninevah	3—A
Nebuchadnezzar subdues Egypt	3—B
Nebuchadnezzar and Tyre	3—C
Alexander and Tyre	3—D
Nature of ancient monarchy	3—E
Balaam's counsel to Midianites and Moabites	3—F
Herod's nationality	3—G
His mad grief for his wife	3—H
His terrible disease	3—I
His dying, wicked designs	3—J
Josephus' testimony concerning Christ	3—K
Concerning John the Baptist	3—L
Herod Agrippa's violent death	3—M
Order, service, and regulation of the high priests	3—N

Misfortunes of Jerusalem, greatest of all times	3—O
Illustration of Heb. 11:37	3—P
Violence of the Romans' engines	3—Q
Reference of hired mourners	3—R
The Sea of Galilee or Gennesareth	3—S
Lake Asphaltitis, or Dead Sea	3—T
Why such vast numbers in siege of Jerusalem	3—U
The "sacrifice and oblation" cease	3—V
Many Jews for sale, but few (or none) to buy	3—W
Jerusalem laid "even with the ground"	3—X
Luther and Lutherianism	3—Y
Petri in Sweden	3—Z
Fredric in Denmark	4—A
Galvin and Galvinistic Baptists	4—B
Knox and Presbyterianism	4—C
Zuingle and the "Reformed Church"	4—D
Fox and the Quakers	4—E
Brown and the Brownists or Congregationalists	4—F
Alexander Mack and the "Brethren" or Dunkards	4—G
Henry VIII and the Church of England	4—H
Wesley and Methodism	4—I
The early churches were independent	4—J
Original power of the bishop	4—K
Power of the bishop increased	4—L
Concentration of power	4—M
Beginning of councils	4—N
Further concentration of power	4—O
Ancient government of the church gone	4—P
Prominence of Rome, Antioch, Alexander and Constantinople	4—Q
Patriarchal form of government	4—R
Supremacy of Rome introduced	4—S
Papal authority increased	4—T
Relation of the church and the state	4—U
Climax, of the power of the pope	4—V
Power of the pope over civil rulers	4—W

Pagan Home "taken away" by Constantine	4—X
Constantine assumes supreme control of church and thus practically unites CHUHCH and STATE	4—Y
The above event increased the power of the already prominent bishops	4—Z
Date of Christ's birth uncertain	5—A
Illustration of last part of Romans 1st chapter	5—B
Origin of private confessional	5—C
Constantine and Sunday	5—D
Sunday the original day of worship	5—E
The first female convent	5—F
The Weddas—Evolution turned around	5—G
Various dates for ascension of Menes	5—H
Chronological table of dates	5—I
A heathen account of the Deluge	5—J
Heathen account of Tower of Babel	5—K
Age of Christ an historical (not mythological) one	5—L
Pliny—Trajan correspodence about the Christians	5—M
Concerning the titles of books of the Bible	5—N
Joint rule of Belshazzar and his father	5—O
Condition of France during revolution	5—P
Sidelights on Acts 23:5	5—Q
Jews cured of idolatry after captivity	5—R
Why Babylonians and Assyrians came "from the north"	5—S
Alexander and the Ptolemies rule in Egypt	5—T
Ptolemy effects the fusion of the races	5—U
Egyptians and Ethiopians taken by Sennacherib	5—V
Curious feature of ancient irrigation	5—W
Papyrus canoes of Egyptians and Ethiopians	5—X
A mother eats a son in the siege	5—Y
Time between canons of Old and New Testaments	5—Z
Statement in Acts 17:21 verified	6—A
Altar TO THE UNKNOWN GOD	6—B
Regulations for transcribers	6—C
Statement in Neh. 8:8 illustrated	6—D
Compiling of books of Old Testament	6—E

Ten general persecutions	6—F
Thickets and banks of the Jordan	6—G
Bowels, seat of passions – ancient theory	6—H
No, or Thebes, in Egypt captured	6—I
Syria, (or Aramea) distinguished from Syria proper	6—J
Birth stools	6—K
Rivers and willows of Babylon	6—L
Darius the Mede, and Cyrus	6—M
The Christian era	10—A and 6—N
New Moon as a beginning date	6—O
Explanatory note on chronology	6—P
Samaritans not idolaters	6—Q
Eater city of Babylon	6—R
Great synagogue	6—S
Old Testament canon compiled	7—Z and 6—S
Mishnah, or traditions	6—S
Proselytes	6—T
Ebionites	6—U
Beating with stripes	6—V
Transmigration of souls	6—W
Herod, his nationality and religion	6—X
Contribution every Sunday	6—Y
Bread and wine for communion	6—Z
Difference between enchanters and preachers	7—A
Church letters	7—B
Infallibility of popes	7—C
Separation, Church and state not thought of by reformers	7—D
Grecians	7—E
Death of Apostle John	7—F
Council of Nice, personnel, and two objects	7—G
Consubstantial? or like-substance	7—H
Horrible persecutions by pagans	7—I
Scriptures no longer authority	7—J
All disciples did not follow apostacy	7—K
Arianism	7—L
Paul's second "defense"	7—M

Martyrdom of Paul and Peter	7—M and 7—N
Peter crucified head downward	7—N
Ignatius' words on his martyrdom	7—O
Noted words of Polycarp	7—P
Length of Christ's ministry	7—Q
Ancients not Sabbath keepers	7—R
Matthew written in Hebrew	7—Z and 7—S
Famous vision of the cross	7—T
Eusebius' estimate of Alexander	7—U
Edict of Constantine for Lord's day	7—V
Bad effects of absence of capital punishment	7—W
Eusebius' description of Ebionism	7—X
Peter ever in Rome?	7—Y
Canon of Old and New Testaments	6—8 and 7—Z
Belshazzar and Nebuchadnezzar, their relation	8—A
Phoenicia, commercial importance of	8—B
Greeks received letters from Phoenicia	8—C
Ahasuerus, identity	8—D
Jewish government (under Romans) in Palestine	8—E
Sojourn of Israelites in Egypt. Length	8—F
Cyrus diverts Euphates and enters Babylon	8—G
Bablyon the greatest city of all	8—H
Tarsus, its riches and importance	8—I
Division of Roman Empire into East and West	8—J
Greek and Roman Churches	8—K
Pope	8—L
Illustration of John 3:8	8—M
Gauls thought human sacrifice necessary	8—N
Canon of Bible and the Church	8—O
Adventists	8—P
Baptists	8—Q
Mennonites	8—R
Mormons	8—S
Universalists	8—T
Episcopal Church, Protestant, in America	8—U
Pouring and sprinkling	8—V

Infant baptism	8—W
Instrumental music in worship	8—X
Sabbath day's journey	8—Y
Modern Sunday—Schools	8—Z
Salvation Army	9—A
I. H. S	9—B
I. N. R. I.	9—C
Protestant, origin of the word	9—D
Massacre of Saint Bartholomew's Day	9—E
Tiberius shares throne with Augustus	9—F
Inscription on fence round Friends church	9—G
Seven hills of Rome	9—H
Christians leave Jerusalem before siege	9—I
Reclining, position while eating	9—J
Religious state of world at advent of Christ	9—K
Uzziah offering incense; earthquake	9—L
Alexander is shown prophecy of Daniel	9—M
Epiphanes desecrates the worship	9—N
Epiphanes; date of his desecration of worship	9—O
Idumeans receive circumcision and become Jews	9—P
Herod; date when he became king of the Jews	9—Q
Cyrenius sent to tax Judea	9—R
Bible and democracy	9—S
Science is destroying religion	9—T
Choirs	9—W and 9—U
Organs	9—V
Congregational singing	9—U and 9—W
Greek Church older and source of Roman	9—X
Image worship—Greek and Roman Churches	9—Y
Twelve hundred years Constantine to Reformation	9—Z
Dionysius Exiguus and the Christian Era	10—A
Brevity of human existence, Gibbon	10—B
Government of Church; a brief taken from Mosheim	10—C
Mohammed; character and personality	10—D
Mohammed; religion and future life	10—E
Christmas	10—F

Easter	10—G
Alexander; did he "sigh for more worlds" etc.?	10—H
Military "glory;" Gibbon's opinion	10—I
Xerxes I. riches; arouses nation against Greece	10—J
Xerxes I. Last Persian ruler of any note	10—K
Alexander's successors; included others besides the "four" noted ones	10—L
Berenice, daughter of Philadelphus, marries Antiochus	10—M
PtolemyIII., Euergetes, comes against Syria	10—N
Ptolemy III, recovers idols of Egypt	10—O
Antichus III., the Great, attacks Egypt	10—P
Ptolemy Philopator defeats Antiochus III	10—Q
Ptolemy Philopator; his pride and arrogance	10—R
Antiochus III. returns against Egypt, stronger	10—S
Ptolemy V. League formed to "stand" against him	10—T
Jews apostatize—selfish motive—failed	10—U
Bobbers of the Jews repulsed	10—V
Antiochus invades Europe; defeated by Romans	10—W
Antiochus' disgraceful death	10—X
Seleueus, "raiser of taxes."	10—Y
Epiphanes' manner of obtaining the crown	10—Z
Epiphanes overcomes the usurper and his friends	11—A
Epiphanes; first expedition against Egypt	11—B
Epiphanes; second expedition into Egypt	11—C
Epiphanes; third expedition into Egypt	11—D
Epiphanes; fourth expedition into Egypt	11—E
Epiphanes' forces desecrate the worship	11—F
Maccabees; accomplished their work with "small" and "little" forces at the beginning	11—G
Epiphanes' attitude toward religion	11—H
Epiphanes' vile and 'despicable character	11—I
Epiphanes' terrible death	11—J
Captivity, Babylonian and Assyrian	11—K
Kings and Chronicles, books of, sources	11—L

HISTORICAL QUOTATIONS

1—A
The People of Mesopotamia worshipped household gods which were images of the gods of the country. It was their custom to carry these gods with them when they traveled into a foreign land. JOSEPHUS, Ant. 18-9-5.

1—B
There were artificial pools in Jerusalem, which were in existence up to the time of the Jewish war. JOSEPHUS, Wars, 5-11-4.

1—C
The Galatians or Gauls were derived from Gomer; and the Medes from Madai, and the Greeks from Javan. JOSEPHUS, Anti. 1-6-1.

1—D
The term "Hebrew" as applied to the Jews, originated from Eber, the son of Salah. JOSEPHUS, Ant. 1-6-4.

1—E
The Arabians circumcise at the 13th year from Ishmael, the founder of their nation. JOSEPHUS, Ant. 1-12-2.

1—F
Josephus enumerates the ten commandments thus: "The first commandment teaches us, that there is but one God, and that we ought to worship only; the second commands us not to make the image of any living creature to worship it; the third, that we must not swear by God in a false matter; the fourth, that we must keep the 7th day, by resting from all sorts of work; the fifth, that we

must honor our parents; the sixth, that we must abstain from murder; the seventh, that we must not commit adultery; the eighth, that we must not be guilty of theft; the ninth, that we must not bear false witness; the tenth, that we must not admit of the desire of any thing that is another's." JOSEPHUS, Ant. 3-5-5.

1—G
The daily sacrifice was congregational, and furnished out of the public money. JOSEPHUS, Ant. 3-10-1.

1—H
The feast of unleavened bread began on the 15th, and the first-fruits came in on the 16th day of the month. The grain was dried before being offered. JOSEPHUS, Ant. 3-10-5.

1—I
When Artaxerxes was about selecting a queen to take the place of Vashti, he had a number of virgins gathered together. These he had to come to him, one each day, with whom he had commerce. JOSEPHUS, Ant. 11-6-2.

1—J
Ptolemy, who received Egypt upon the division of Alexander's empire, carried many of the Jews into Egypt. JOSEPHUS, Ant. 12-1-1.

1—K
Ptolemy Philadelphus has the Hebrew Scriptures translated into the Greek tongue. For this purpose he employed learned men out of the Jewish nation. JOSEPHUS, Ant. 12-2-1.

1—L
Certain Jews once became dissatisfied with the treatment they received from other Jews and appeared to Antiochus. Under his protection they built a gymnasium at Jerusalem. This was a place where the exercises were performed naked; and as they wished to

repudiate the Jewish customs, they here resorted to a certain trick whereby they hid the mark of circumcision, thus practically "becoming uncircumcised." JOSEPHUS, Ant. 12-5-1.

1—M
After the division of Alexander's empire, and the subsequent oppression of the Jews in Judea, Onias, the high-priest, fled to Alexandria in Egypt. While there he obtained leave of Ptolemy, and built an altar and temple like the one at Jerusalem. JOSEPHUS, Ant. 13-3-1.

1—N
One great difference between the Pharisees and Sadducees was that the former held a great many observances by succession from their fathers which are not written in the law, while the latter rejected everything that is not written therein. JOSEPHUS, Ant. 13-10-6.

    MOSHEIM, B, 1, P, 1. C. 2, S. 7

1—O
In the days of the Maccabees, the Jews revolted from their oppressors, conducted successful warfare, and enjoyed a period of comparative independence. JOSEPHUS, Ant. 12-6-1 to 14-16-4.

1—P
This independence of the Jews ended when Pompey took Jerusalem. This was occasioned by the seditious conduct of Hyrcanus and Aristobulus (rival brothers) toward each other. The period had lasted 126 years, and was succeeded by Herod the Great. JOSEPHUS, Ant. 14-4-4 and 14-16-4.

1—Q
It was unlawful to kill, even a wicked man, until he had been condemned by the Sanhedrin at Jerusalem. On this account no

one could perish, lawfully, outside of Jerusalem. JOSEPHUS, Ant, 14-9-3.

1—R
"From the remotest times the city-states of Babylonia had for their enemies the kings of Elam, a country bordering Babylonia on the east, and of which Susa was the capital. Their dominion was finally broken by a king of Babylon, a city which had been gradually rising into prominence, and which was to give to the whole country the name by which it is best known, Babylonia. The name of this king was Hammurabi. He united under his rule all the cities of Babylonia and became the true founder of what is known as the Old (or early) Babylonian Empire." MYERS, Ancient History, p. 50.

1—S
"Meanwhile (see above) a Semitic power had been slowly developing in the north. This was the Assyrian Empire, the later heart and center of which was the great city of Ninevah. For a long time Assyria was practically a province of the lower kingdom; but in 728 B. C., Babylonia was conquered by an Assyrian king (Tiglath Pileser) and from that time on to 625 B. C., the country was for the most part under Assyrian control." MYERS, Ancient History. p. 51.

1—T
Saracus was the last king of the Assyrians. Various powers began now to rebel against the proud and oppressing court of Ninevah. Nabopolassar, who was a vassal king of this court, took advantage of its declining strength and revolted. He later founded the Later Babylonian Empire. MYERS, Ancient History, pp. 66, 72.

1—U
Medes and Persians are names of people who sought homes on the plateau of Iran. Those who settled in the south were called Persians. Those in the northwest were called Medes. It seems on

account of their common origin their names were closely associated.

These people were coming into prominence in course of the days of the Later Babylonian Empire. MYERS, Ancient History, pp. 73, 88.

1—V
The Medes were at first the leading race, but their greatness was of a short duration. The Persians, under Cyrus, overthrew their power and obtained control, and thus originated the Medo-Persian Empire. MYERS, Ancient History, pp. 88, 89 HERODOTUS 1-130.

1—W
The Babylonian Empire which was founded by Nabopolassar, continued until Belshazzar, when it was overthrown by the Medo-Persian under Cyrus. MYERS, Ancient History, pp 73, 89, 90.

1—X
The Persian Empire was followed by the Macedonian. Alexander the Great of Macedon, conducted an army across the continent of Asia, subjugating the Persian dominions, and on their ruins founded the short-lived Macedon Empire. MEYRS, Ancient History, pp. 93, 275-285.

1—Y
Alexander accomplished the conquest of the vast dominions of the Persian Empire in no more than 12 years. He swept across the country of the "Great King" with such rapid success that it might well be called a "flying trip." MYERS, Ancient History, pp. 275, 282, 286.

1—Z
There was no one strong enough to fill the place of Alexander, or "stand up in his power," MYERS, Ancient History, p 286.

2—A
After Alexander's death, his monarchy fell apart, and four others arose therefrom. MYERS, A. M., p. 287. ROLLIN, Vol 1, p, 140. JOSEPHUS, Ant. 12-1-1.

2—B
"We have seen that after the death of Alexander, his empire was divided, and weakened by internal wars. Meanwhile, a hitherto obscure city (Rome) was reaching out and increasing in extent and power. This wonderful power continued to engross one people after another until the fragments of Alexander's empire and practically all the world were brought under her sway. Thus, was formed the Roman Empire." MYERS, A. H., pp. 367-474.

2—C
The Roman Empire was the most thoroughly organized of any in ancient history. "It was not a loose aggregation of states, ready to fall apart as soon as the hand that fettered them was removed, but an empire carefully welded together, building up in every land its own civilization, and developing a national unity which held its possessions together for a thousand years." Its strength was iron-like. RAND McNALLY BIBLE ATLAS, p. 97.

2—D
"After Psammetichus had passed some years there, waiting for a favorable opportunity to revenge himself for the affront which had been put upon him, a courier brought his advice, that brazen men had landed in Egypt. These were Grecian soldiers. Carions and lonians, who had been cast upon the coast of Egypt by a storm, and were completely covered with helmets, cuirasses, and other arms of brass." ROLLIN, V. 1, p. 223. HERODOTUS 2-152.

2—E
The "River of Egypt" mentioned as the boundary between Palestine and Egypt, was not the Nile, but a small river running

throughout the desert that lay' between those two nations. ROLLIN, V. 1, p 228 and note. PRIDEAUX. Ano. 605.

2—F
"The family from which I am derived is not an ignoble one, but hath descended all along from the priests and as nobility among several people is of a different origin, so with us to be the sacerdotal dignity, is an indication of the splendor of a family." JOSEPHUS— Life, Sec. 1.

2—G
The original color of the earth was red. The word Adam in the Hebrew tongue means "one who is red." JOSEPHUS, Ant. B. 1, C. 1, S. 2.

2—H
"He also deprived the serpent of speech, out of indignation at his malicious disposition towards Adam. Besides this, he inserted poison under his tongue, and made him an enemy of man; and suggested to them that they should direct their strokes against his head, that being the place wherein lay his malicious designs toward men, and it being easiest to take vengeance on him that way. And when he had deprived him of the use of his feet, and made him go rolling all along, and dragging himself upon the ground." JOSEPHUS, Ant. 1-1-4.

2—I
The midwives employed in the time of the oppression were Egyptians instead of Hebrews, according to Josephus. Ant. 2-9-2.

2—J
"But as for the Arabians, they circumcise after the 13 year, because Ishmael, the founder of their nation, who was born to Abraham by the concubine, was circumcised at that age." JOSEPHUS, Ant. 1-12-2.

2—K
"Soon after the bright period of the twelfth dynasty, Egypt again suffered a great eclipse. Nomadic Tribes from Asia pressed across the eastern frontier of Egypt and gradually took possession of the inviting pasture lands of the delta, and established there the empire of the Shepherd Kings. These. Asiatic intruders were violent and barbarous, and destroyed or mutilated the monuments of the country." MYERS, A. H., p. 26.

2—L
"As was I born to Matthias in the first year of the reign of Caius Caesar. I have three sons: Hyrcanus, the eldest, was born in the 4th year of the reign of Vespasian, as was Justus born in the 7th, and Agrippa in the 9th." JOSEPHUS—Life, Sec. 1.

2—M
The Passover lamb was killed on the 14th, the feast of unleavened bread begun on the 15th, and the first-fruits were offered on the 16th day of the month. JOSEPHUS, Ant. 3-10-5,

2—N
Josephus says Lot's daughters were betrothed. Ant. 1-11-4. He says that Hyrcanus "was Herod's father-in-law already" (14-13-1), and yet later (S-6) says "whose daughter he had espoused." From this it is seen that in ancient times an espousal was spoken of as a marriage.

2—O
"Now these thirteen (H. priests) who were the descendants of two of the sons of Aaron, received this dignity by succession, one after another." JOSEPHUS, Ant. 20-10-1.

2—P
The Egyptians were ardent. worshippers of animals; among them the bull Apis was the most famous. This fact suggested the golden

calf to the Israelites who had been with them so long. ROLLIN, V. 1, p. 184.

2—Q
Ancient Babylon was very imposingly built. It was walled up four-square. One each of the four sides were 25 gates. These were of brass... The Euphrates ran through the city, both of its banks being walled securely. These walls opened to each street running to them with gates of brass. It was the custom to have these gates open in day time but closed at night. ROLLIN, V. 1, pp. 448, 449.

2—R
"At the same time that Antiochus, who was called Epiphanes, (who was king of Syria after the division of Alexander's empire) had a quarrel with the 5th Ptolemy about his right to the whole country of Syria, a great sedition fell among the men of power in Judea, and they had a contention about obtaining the government; while each of those that were of dignity could not endure to be subject to their equals. However, Onias, one of the high-priests, got the better, and east the sons of Tobias out of the city; who fled to Antiochus, and besought him to make use of them for his leaders, and to make an expedition into Judea. The king being thereto disposed before hand, complied with them, and came upon the Jews with a great army, and took their city by force, and slew a great multitude of those who favored Ptolemy, and sent out his soldiers to plunder them, without mercy. He also spoiled the temple and put a stop to the constant practice of offering a daily sacrifice of expiation, for three years and 6 months." JOSEPHUS, Ant. 12-5-4. Wars, 1-1-1.

2—S
"When this concern about these affairs were added to the former, he (Epiphanes) was confounded, and, by the anxiety he was in, fell into a distemper, which, as it lasted a great while, and his pains increased upon him, so he at length perceived he should die in a little time; so he called his friends to him, and told them that

his distemper was sore upon him, and confessed withal, that this calamity was sent upon him for the miseries he had brought upon the Jewish nation, while he plundered their temple and condemned their God; and when he had said this lie gave up the ghost." JOSEPHUS, Ant. 12-9-1.

2—T
"It then happened that Cestius was not conscious either how the besieged despaired of success, nor how courageous the people were for him; and so he recalled his soldiers from the place, and by despairing of any expectation of taking it, without having received any disgrace, he retired from the city, without any reason in the world." While Josephus could see no reason yet it was doubtless the hand of God causing the retreat, to give the Christians in the city opportunity to heed the warning of Christ to flee to the mountains for safety. This they did on this occasion and were preserved. JOSEPHUS, Wars, 2-19-6, 7 and note HORNE Introduction V. 1, p. 460.

2—U
"Then came the ensigns encompassing the eagle, which is at the head of every Roman legion, the king and the strongest of all birds, which seems to them a signal of dominion, and an omen that they shall conquer all against whom they march." JOSEPHUS, Wars, 3-6-2.

2—V
"It may be worth our while to observe here, that near this lake of Gennesaret grapes and figs hang on the trees ten months of the year. We may observe also, that in Cyril of Jerusalem, Catechus, 18, see. 3, which was delivered not long before Easter, there were no fresh leaves of fig trees, nor bunches of fresh grapes in Judea, so that when St. Mark says: (11:13) that our Saviour, soon after the same time of the year, came and 'found leaves' on a fig tree near Jerusalem, but 'no figs,' because the time of 'new figs' ripening 'was not yet,' he says very true; nor were they therefore other

than old leaves which our Saviour saw, and old figs which he expected, and which even with us commonly hang on the trees all winter long." NOTE on Josephus. Wars, 3-10-8.

2—W
The troubles of the people of Jerusalem during the war were many and great for they were divided into three seditious factions, (Josephus, Wars, 5-1-1) provisions were wantonly destroyed, (5-1-4) they ate corn unground and uncooked, (5-10-2) children would snatch the last morsel from the parent, and the mother from the infant. Children were lifted from the ground by the food they held in the mouth. People were beaten who ate their own food before the robbers arrived. Those who were suspected of having hidden some food were tortured by having sharp stakes driven up their fundamentals, (5-10-3) and the famine consumed whole families. Many died as they were burying others. There was no lamentation as the famine confounded all natural passions. A stupefying silence and awe overcame them (5-12-3). Some had swallowed their money, and then had their bodies ripped open by robbers (5-14-4). Some searched the sewers and dung-piles for food (5-13-7) and ate hay, old shoes and leather (6-3-3). A mother roasted and ate her son (6-3-4); bloodshed was so great as to quench the fire in the houses (6-8-5).

2—X
"Now the warlike men that were in the city, and the multitude of the seditious that were with Simon, were ten thousand, besides the Idumeans. Those ten thousand had fifty commanders, over whom this Simon was supreme. The Idumean that paid him homage were five thousand, and had eight commanders, among whom those of greatest fame were Jacob, the son of Sosas, and Simon, the son of Cathlas. John, who had seized upon the temple, had six thousand armed men, under twenty commanders; the Zealots also that had come over to him, and left off their opposition, were two thousand four hundred, and had the same commander they had formerly, Eleazer, together with Simon the son

12 | *Historical Quotations*

of Ariens. Now while the factions fought one against another, the people were their prey, on both sides, as we have said already; and that part of the people who would not join with them in their wicked practices, were plundered by both factions. Simon held the upper city, and the great wall as far as Cedron, and as much of the old wall as bent from Siloam to the east, and which went down to the palaces of Monobazus, who was king of the Adiabeni, beyond Euphrates. He also held that fountain and the Aera, which was no other than the lower city; he also held all that reached to the palace of queen Helena, the mother of Monobazua; but John held the temple, and the parts thereto adjoining, for a great way, as also Opila, and the valley called 'the Valley of Cedron'; and when the parts that were interposed between their possessions were burnt by them, they left a space wherein they might fight with each other; for this internal sedition did not cease even when the Romans were encamped near their very walls. But although they had grown wiser at the first onset the Romans had made upon them, this lasted but a while; for they returned to their former madness, and separated one from another; and fought it out and did every thing that the besiegers could desire them to do; for they never suffered anything that was worse from the Romans than they made each other, suffer, nor was there any misery endured by the city after these men's actions that could be esteemed new. But it was most of all unhappy before it was overthrown, while those that took it did it a greater kindness; for I venture to affirm, that the sedition destroyed the city, and the Romans destroyed the sedition, which it was a much harder thing to do than to destroy the walls; so that we may justly ascribe our misfortunes to our own people and the just vengeance taken on them to the Romans." JOSEPHUS, Wars, 5-6-1. See also entire first chapter of Book 5.

2—Y
Concerning the complete destruction of the city of Babylon, Rollin says: "In the first place, Babylon ceased to be a royal city, the kings of Persia choosing to reside elsewhere. They delighted

more in Shushan, Ecbatana, Persepolis, or any other place, and did themselves destroy a great part of Babylon. . . . The new kings of Persia, who afterwards became masters of Babylon, completed the ruin of it, by building Ctesiphon, which carried away all the remainder of the inhabitants. . . . She was totally forsaken, that nothing of her was left remaining but the walls. And to this condition was she reduced at the time when Persians wrote his remarks upon Greece. . . The kings of Persia, finding the place deserted, made a park of it, in which they kept wild beasts for hunting. . . . Instead of citizens, it was now inhabited by wild boars, leopards, bears, deer and wild asses. Babylon was now the retreat of fierce, savage, deadly creatures, that hate the light, and delight in darkness. . . . But it was still too much that the walls of Babylon were still standing. At length, they fell down in several places, and were never repaired. Various accidents destroyed the remainder. The animals, which served for pleasure for the Persian kings, abandoned the place; serpents and scorpions remained, so that it became a dreadful place for persons that should have curiosity to visit, or search after its antiquities. The Euphrates that used to run through the city, having no longer a free channel, took its course another way; so that, in Theodoret's time, there was but a very little stream of water left, which ran across the ruins, and, not meeting with a descent or free passage, necessarily expanded into a marsh. In the time of Alexander the Great the river had left its ordinary channel, by reason of the outlets and canals which Cyrus had made, and of which we already have given an account; these outlets, being all stopped up, had occasioned a great inundation in the country, Alexander, designing to fix the seat of his empire at Babylon, projecting the bringing back the Euphrates into its natural and former channel and had actually set his men to work. But the Almighty, who watched over the fulfilling of his prophecy, defeated this enterprise by the death of Alexander, which happened soon after. It is easy to comprehend how, after this, Babylon being neglected lo such a degree as we have seen, its river was converted into an in accessible pool. . . By means of all these changes, Babylon became an utter dessert, and all the country around fell into the same state of desolation and horror; so that the ablest geographers at this day (A. D. 1729) can not determine the place where it stood." ROLLINS, V. 1, pp. 558-560.

2—Z
The feast of Bacchus was a feast of the Greeks, held in honor of Bacchus, "The God of Wine." The public were entertained with games, shows, and dramatic representations. These feasts continued many days. Those who were initiated, mimicked whatever the poets had thought fit to feign of the god Bacchus. They covered themselves with skin of wild beasts, carried a thyrsus in their hands, a kind of pik with ivy leaves twisted round it. . . Men and women, ridiculously transformed in this manner, appeared night and day in public, and imitating drunkenness, and dancing with the most indecent postures ran in throngs about the mountains and forests, screaming and howling furiously. . . . To these ceremonies others were added, obscene to the last excess. . . . Nothing was seen but dancing, drunkenness, debauchery, and all that the most abandoned licentiousness could conceive." ROLLIN, V. 1, pp. 45, 46 BRITANNICA, V. 7, p. 247 and V. 17, p. 839.

3—A
"Saracus, who came to the throne towards the end of the 7th century B. C., was the last of the long line of Assyrian kings. For nearly or quite six centuries the Ninevite kings had now lorded it over the East. There was scarcely a state in all Western Asia that during this time had not, in the language of the royal inscriptions 'borne the heavy yoke of their lordship' scarcely a people that had not suffered their cruel punishments, or tasted the bitterness of enforced exile. But now swift misfortunes were bearing down upon the oppressor from every quarter. Egypt revolted and tore Syria away from the empire; from the mountains defiles on the east issued the armies of the recent-grown empire of the Aryan Medes, led by the renowned Cyaxares; from the southern lowlands, anxious to aid in the overthrow of the hated oppressor, the Babylonians joined the Medes as allies, and together they' laid

close siege to Ninevah. The city' was finally taken and sacked, and dominion passed away forever from the proud capitol two hundred years later, when Xenophon with his Ten Thousand Greeks, in his memorable retreat passed the spot, the once great city was a crumbling mass of ruins of which he could not even learn the name." MYERS, A. H., p. 66. BRITANNICA, V. 18, p. 563, Article—Persia.

3—B
"The king of Babylon, taking advantage therefore of the intestine divisions which the rebellion of Amasis had occasioned in that kingdom, marched thither at the head of his army. He subdued Egypt from Migdol or Magdol, a town on the frontiers of the kingdom, as far as Syene, in the opposite extremity where it borders on Ethiopia. He made a horrible devastation wherever he came; killed a great number of the inhabitants, and made such dreadful havoc in the country, that the damage could not be repaired in forty years. Nebuchadnezzar, having loaded his army with spoils, and conquered the whole kingdom, came to an accommodation with Amasis; and leaving him as his viceroy there, returned to Babylon." ROLLIN, V. 1, p. 232. Britannica, V. 7, p. 743, Article—Egypt. Josephus, Ant. 10-9-7 and 10-10-3.

3—C
"With Jerusalem subdued, Nebuchadnezzar pushed with all his force the siege of the Phoenician city of Tyre, whose investment had been commenced several years before. In striking language the prophet Ezekiel (29-18) describes the length and hardness of the siege: 'every head was made bald, and every shoulder was peeled.' After thirteen years Nebuchadnezzar was apparently forced to raise the siege." MYERS A. H, p. 72. "Nebuchadnezzar laid siege to the great merchant-city, (Tyre) which was still rich and strong enough to hold out for thirteen years. Ezekiel says that Nebuchadnezzar and his host had no reward for their heavy service against Tyre, and the presumption is that the city capitulated on favorable terms." BRITANNICA, V. 18, p. 808. "Accordingly,

at the time we are speaking of, she (Tyre) was in a condition to resist, thirteen years together, a monarch to whose yoke all the rest of the East had submitted. It was not till after so many years that Nebuchadnezzar made himself master of Tyre. His troops suffered incredible hardships before it; so that, according to the prophet's expression, 'every head was made bald, and every shoulder was peeled.' Before the city was reduced to the last extremity, its inhabitants retired, with the greatest part of their effects, into a neighboring isle, half a mile from the shore, where they built a new city; the name and glory of which extinguished the remembrance of the old one, which from thenceforward became a mere village, retaining the name of ancient Tyre. Nebuchadezzar and his army having undergone the utmost fatigues during so long and difficult a siege, and having found, nothing in the place to requite them for the service they had rendered to Almighty God in executing his vengeance upon the city, God was pleased to promise by the mouth of Ezekiel that he would give them the spoils of Egypt for a recompense." ROLLIN, V, 1, p. 472. See also Josephus, Ant. 10-11-1 and Against. Apion, 1-21.

3—D
"The Tyrians also offered submission, but refused to allow Alexander to enter the city and sacrifice in the temple of Hercules. Alexander was determined to make an example of the first sign of opposition that did not proceed from Persian officials, and at once began the siege. It lasted seven months, and, though the king, with enormous toil, drove a mole from the mainland to the island, he made little progress till the Persians were mad enough to dismiss the fleet and give him command of the sea through his Cyprian and Phoenician allies. The town was at length forced in July, 332; 8000 Tyrians were slain, 30,000 inhabitants sold as slaves, and only a few notables . . . were spared. Tyre thus lost its political existence, and the foundation of Alexandria, presently changed the lines of trade and gave a blow perhaps still more fatal to the Phoenician cities." BRITANNICA, V. 18, p. 809. MYERS, A. H., p. 275. Josephus, Ant. 11-8-3. Rollin, V. 3, pp. 187-204.

3—E
"The modern system of centralized organization by which the various provinces of a vast empire are cemented into a compact mass, was unknown to the ancient world, and has never been practiced by Asiatics. The satrapical system of government, or that in which the provinces retain their individuality, but are administered on a common plan by officers appointed by the crown —which has prevailed generally through the East since the time of its first introduction—was the invention of Darius Hystaspis. Before his time the greatest monarchies had a slighter and weaker organization. They were in all eases composed of a number of separate kingdoms each under its own native king; and the sole link uniting them together and constituting them an empire, was the subjection of these petty monarchs to a single suzerain. The Babylonian, Assyrian, Median, and Lydian, were all empires of this type—monarchies, wherein a sovereign prince at the head of a powerful kingdom was acknowledged as suzerain by a number of inferior princes, each in his own right sole ruler of his own country. And the subjection of the inferior princes consisted chiefly, if not solely, in two points; they were bound to render homage to their suzerain, and to pay him annually a certain stated tribute." RAWLINSON, Historical Evidences, Page 95.

3—F
When Balaam at last did not curse Israel, Balak was angry and sent him away without any honors. But he was scarcely on his journey when he sent for Balak and the princes of the Midianites and conferred with them to the injury of the Israelites. He told them that no complete destruction could befall the Israelites, for God was with them; but that small misfortunes might be brought against them if they would follow his advice. Whereupon he advised them to select their handsomest daughters—those most eminent for beauty, and the most proper for conquering the passions of men, and to deck them to the highest degree. And then to "send them to be near the Israelites' camp and give them in charge, that when the young men of the Hebrews desire their

company, they allow it them; and when they see that they are enamored of them, let them take their leaves; and if they entreat them to stay, let them not give their consent till they have persuaded them to leave off their obedience to their own laws and the worship of that God who established them, and to worship the gods of the Midianites and Moabites; for by this means God will be angry at them. Accordingly, when Balaam had suggested this counsel to them, he went his way." And this counsel was received favorably by the Midianites and Moabites, who proceeded to put it into practice. For they sent their daughters to be near the Hebrews, whose young men were taken with their beauty, and were led to Seek their company. And so completely were they overcome by their passion for the young women, that they agreed to forsake their own God and worship the gods of the Midianites, in order to retain the company of them. JOSEPHUS 4-6-6, 7, 8, 9.

3—G
"But Antigonus, by way of reply to what Herod had caused to be proclaimed, and this before the Romans, and before Silo also, said, that they would not do justly if they gave the kingdom to Herod, who was not more than a private man, and an Idumean, i.e., a half Jew." JOSEPHUS 14-15-2.

3—H
"But when she was once dead, the king's affections for her were kindled in a more outrageous manner than before, whose old passion for her we have already described; for his love to her was not of a calm nature, nor such as we usually meet with among other husbands; for at its commencement it was of an enthusiastic kind; nor was it, by their long cohabitation and free conversation together brought under his power to manage; but at this time his love to Marianne seemed to seize him in such a peculiar manner, as looked like divine vengeance upon him for the taking away of her life; for he would frequently call for her, and frequently lament for her, in a most indecent manner. Moreover, he

bethought him of every thing he could make use of to divert his mind from thinking of her, and contrived feasts and assemblies for that purpose, but nothing would suffice; he therefore laid aside his administration of public affairs, and was so far conquered by his passion, that he would order his servants to call for Marianne, as if she were still alive, and could still hear them." JOSEPHUS 15-7-7.

3—I
"But now Herod's distemper greatly increased upon him after a severe manner, and this by God's judgment upon him for his sins; for a fire glowed in him slowly, which did not much appear to the touch outwardly as it augmented his pains inwardly; for it brought upon him a vehement appetite for eating, which he could not avoid to supply with one sort of food or other. His entrails were also exulcerated, and the chief violence of his pain lay in his colon; an aqueous and transparent liquor also settled itself about his feet, and a like matter afflicted him at the bottom of his abdomen. . . . and when, he sat upright he had a difficulty of breathing, which was very loathsome, on account of the stench of his breath, and the quickness of its returns; he had also convulsions in all parts of his body, which increased his strength to an insufferable degree." JOSEPHUS 17-6-5.

3—J
"Though he (Herod) were near his death, he contrived the following wicked designs. He commanded that all the principal men of the entire nation wheresoever they lived, should be called to him. Accordingly, there was a great number that came, because the whole nation was called, and all men heard of this call, and death was the penalty of such as should despise the epistles that were sent to call them. And now the king was in a wild rage against them all, the innocent as well as those that had afforded him ground for accusations; and when they were come, he ordered them all to be shut up in the hippodrome (race track) and sent for his sister Salome, and her husband Alexas, and spoke thus to

them: 'I shall die in a little time, so great are my pains; which death ought to be cheerfully borne, and to be welcomed by all men; but what principally troubles me is this, that I shall die without being lamented, and without such mourning as men usually expect at a king's death. For that he was not unacquainted with the temper of the Jews, that his death would be a thing very desirable, and exceedingly acceptable to them; because during his lifetime they were ready to revolt from him, and to abuse the donations he had dedicated to God; that it therefore was their business to resolve to afford him some alleviation of his great sorrows on this occasion; for that, if they did not refuse him their consent in what he desires, he shall have a great mourning at his funeral, and such as never any king had before him; for then the whole nation would mourn from their very soul, which otherwise Would be done in sport and mockery only. He desired therefore that as soon as they see he has given up the ghost, they shall place soldiers round the hippodrome, while they do not know that he is dead, and that they shall not declare his death to the multitude till this is done, but that they shall give orders to have those that are in custody shot with their darts; and that this slaughter of them all will cause that he shall not miss to rejoice on a double account; that as he is dying, they will make his secure that his will shall be executed in what he charges them to do; and that he shall have the honor of a memorable mourning at his funeral." JOSEPHUS, Ant. 17-6-5.

3—K
"Now, there was about this time Jesus, a wise man, if it be lawful to call him a man, for he was a doer of wonderful works, a teacher of such men as receive the truth with pleasure. He drew over to him both many of the Jews and many of the Gentiles. He was (the) Christ; and when Pilate at the suggestion of the principal men amongst us, had condemned him to the cross, for he appeared to them alive again the third day, as the divine prophets had foretold these and ten thousand other wonderful things con-

cerning him; and the tribe of Christians, so named from him, are not extinct at this day." JOSEPHUS, Ant. 18-3-3.

3—L
"Now, some of the Jews thought that the destruction of Herod's army came from God, and that very justly, as punishment of what he did against John, that was called the Baptist; for Herod slew him, who was a good man, and commanded the Jews to exercise virtue, both as to righteousness towards one another, and piety towards God, and so to come to baptism; for that the washing (with water) would be acceptable to him, if they made use of it, not in order to the putting away (or the remission) of some sins (only) but for the purification of the body." JOSEPHUS, Ant. 18-5-2.

3—M
"Now, when (Herod) Agrippa had reigned three years over all Judea, he came to the city Caesarea, which was formerly called Strato's Tower; and there he exhibited shows in honor of Caesar. . . . On the second day of which shows he put on a garment made wholly of silver, and of a contexture truly wonderful, and came into the theatre early in the morning; at which time the silver of his garment being illuminated by the fresh reflection of the sun's ray upon it, shone out after a surprising manner, and was so resplendent as to spread a horror over those that looked intently upon him; and presently his flatterers cried out, one from one place, and another from another (though not for his good), that he was a god; and they added, 'Be thou merciful to us; for although we have hitherto reverenced thee only as a man, yet shall we henceforth own thee as superior to mortal nature.' Upon this the king neither rebuke them nor reject their impious flattery. But presently. . . . into the deepest sorrow, a severe pain also arose in his abdomen, and began in a most violent manner. . . When he had said this, his pain was become violent,. . . . And when he had been quite worn out by the pain in his abdomen for five days, he

departed this life, being in the 54th year of his age, and in the 7th year of his reign." JOSEPHUS, Ant. 19-8-2.

3—N
"And now I think it proper and agreeable to this history, to give an account of our high priests; how they began, who those are which are capable of that dignity, and how many of them there had been at the end of the war. In the first place, therefore, history informs us that Aaron, the brother of Moses, officiated to God as a high-priest; and that, after his death, his sons succeeded him immediately; and that this dignity hath been continued down from them all to their posterity. Whence it is a custom of our country, that no one should take the high-priesthood of God, but he that is of the blood of Aaron, while every one that is of another stock, though he were a king, can never obtain that high-priesthood. Accordingly, the number of all the high-priests from Aaron, of whom we have spoken already as of the first of them, until Phanas, who was made high-priest during the war by the seditious, was eighty-three of whom thirteen officiated as high-priests in the wilderness, from the days of Moses, while the tabernacle was standing, until the people came into Judea, when King Solomon erected the temple of God; for at first they held the high-priesthood to the end of their life, although afterward they had successors while they were alive. Now these thirteen, who were the descendants of two of the sons of Aaron, received this dignity by succession, one after another." JOSEPHUS, Ant. 20-10-1.

3—O
"Because it had so come to pass, that our city Jerusalem had arrived at a higher degree of felicity than any other city under the Roman government, and yet at last fell into the sorest calamities again. Accordingly it appears to me, that the misfortune of all men, from the beginning of the world, if they be compared to these of the Jews, are not so considerable as they were; while the

authors of them were not foreigners neither." JOSEPHUS, Wars; Pref. Sec. 4,

3—P
"However, Josephus contrived another stratagem besides the foregoing, to get plenty of what they wanted. There was a certain rough and uneven place that could hardly be ascended, and on that account was not guarded by the soldiers; so he sent out certain persons along the western part of the valley, and by them sent letters to whom he pleased of the Jews that were out of the city, and procured from them what necessaries soever they wanted in the city of abundance; he enjoined them also to keep generally along by the watch as they came into the city, and to cover their backs with such sheep skins as had their wool upon them, that if any should spy them in the night they might be believed to be dogs. This was done till the watch perceived their stratagem, and encompassed that rough place about themselves." JOSEPHUS; Wars, 3-7-14.

3—Q
"For the force with which these engines threw stones and darts made them hurt several at a time and, the violent noise of the stones that were cast by the engines was so great, that they carried away the pinnacles of the wall, and broke off the corners of the tower; for no body of men could be so strong as not to be overthrown to the last rank by the largeness of the stones; and any one may learn the force of the engines by what happened this very night; for as one of those that stood round about Josephus was near the wall, his head was carried away by such a stone, and his skull was flung as far as three furlongs. In the day time also, a woman with child had her abdomen so violently struck as she was just come out of her house that the infant was carried to the distance of half a furlong; so great was the force of that engine." JOSEPHUS, Wars, 3-7-23.

3—R
"And some mourned for those that had lived with them, others for their kindred, others for their friends, and others for their brethren, but all mourned for Josephus; insomuch that the lamentation did not cease in the city before the thirtieth day; and a great many hired mourners with their pipes, who should begin the melancholy duties for them." JOSEPHUS, Wars, 3-9-5.

3—S
"Now the lake of Gennesaret is so called from the country adjoining to it. Its breadth is forty furlongs, and its length one hundred and forty. Its waters are sweet and very agreeable for drinking, for they are finer than the thick waters of other fens; the lake is also pure, and on every side ends directly at the shores and at the sand; it is also of a temperate nature when you draw it up, and of a more-gentle nature than river or fountain water, and yet always cooler than one could expect in so diffuse a place as this is. Now when this water is kept in the open air it is as cold as that snow which the country people are accustomed to make by night in summer. There are several kinds of fish in it, different both to the taste and the sight from those elsewhere; it is divided into two parts by the river Jordan. Now Panium is thought to be the fountain of Jordan, but in reality it is carried thither after an occult manner from the place called Phiala. This place lies as you go up to Trachonitis, and is a hundred and twenty furlongs from Caesarea, and is not far out of the road on the right hand." JOSEPHUS, Wars, 3-10-7.

3—T
"The nature of the lake Asphaltites is also worth describing. It is, as I have said already, bitter and unfruitful. It is so light or thick that it bears up the heaviest things that are thrown into it; nor is it easy for anyone to make things sink therein to the bottom, if he had a mind so to do. Accordingly, when Vespasian went to see it, he commanded that some who could not swim, should have their hands tied behind them, and be thrown into the deep, when it so

happened that they all swam as if a wind had forced them upward. Moreover, the change of the color of this lake is wonderful, for it changes its appearance twice every day; and as the rays of the sun fall differently' upon it, the light is variously reflected. However, it casts up black clods of bitumen in many parts of it; these swim at the top of it and resemble both in shape and bigness headless bulls; and when the laborers that belong to the lake come to it, and catch hold of it as it hangs together, they draw it into their ships; but when the ship is full, it is not easy to cut off the rest, for it is so tenacious as to make the ship hang upon its clods till they let it loose with the. . . . blood of women, and with, to which alone it yields. . . . The country of Sodom borders upon it. . . . It is related how, for the impiety of its inhabitants, it was burnt with lightning. In consequence of which there are still the remainders of that divine fire; and the traces, or shadows, of the five cities are still to be seen, as well as the ashes growing in their fruits, which fruits have a color as if they were fit to be eaten; but if you pluck them with your hands, they will dissolve into smoke and ashes. And thus, what is related of this land, of Sodom hath these marks of credibility which our very sight affords us." JOSEPHUS, Wars, 4-8-4.

3—U
"Now the number of those that were carried captive during this whole war was collected to be 97,000; as was the number of those that perished during the siege 1,100,000 the greater part of whom were indeed of the same nation with the citizens of Jerusalem, but not belonging to the city itself; for they were come up from all the country to the feast of unleavened bread; and were, on a sudden shut up by an army, which, at the very first, occasioned so great a straightness among them that there came a pestilential destruction upon them, and soon afterward such a famine as destroyed them more suddenly." JOSEPHUS, Wars, 6-9-3.

3—V
"While he (Titus) himself had Josephus brought to him (for he had been informed that on that very day, which was the 17th day of Panemus, or Tamus, the sacrifice called 'The Daily Sacrifice' had failed, and had not been offered to God for want of men to offer it, and that the people were grievously troubled at it), and commanded him" etc. JOSEPHUS, Wars, 6-2-1.

3—W
"These were all received by the Romans, because Titus himself grew negligent as to his former orders for killing them, and because the very soldiers grew weary of killing them, and because they hoped to get some money by sparing them; for they left only the populace, and sold the rest of the multitude, with their wives and. children, and every one of them at a very low price, and that because such as were sold were very many, and the buyers very few." JOSEPHUS, Wars, 6-8-2.

3—X
"But for all the rest of the wall, it was so thoroughly laid even with the ground by those that dug it up to the foundation that there was left nothing to make those that came thither believe it had ever been inhabited. This was the end that Jerusalem came to by the madness of those that were for innovations; a city otherwise of great magnificence, and of mighty fame among all mankind." JOSEPHUS, Wars 7-1-1.

3—Y
Lutherans are that body of Christians who adopted the principles of Martin Luther in his opposition to the Roman Church, to the Swiss theologians, and to the sectaries of Reformation times. They called themselves 'Evangelical' in distinction from the 'Reformed' or followers of Calvin, and formed one of the two great divisions of the Reformation Church." Britannica, V. 15, Article—Lutherans. "While the Roman pontiff slumbered in security at the head of the church, and saw nothing throughout the vast

extent of his dominion but tranquility and submission; and while the worthy and pious professors of genuine Christianity almost despaired of seeing that reformation on which their most ardent desires and expectations were bent; an obscure and inconsiderable person suddenly offered himself to public view in 1617, and laid the foundation of this long expected change, by opposing, with undaunted resolution, his single force to the torrent of papal ambition and despotism. This extraordinary man was Martin Luther a native of Eisleben in Saxony, a monk of the Augustinian Eremites, (one of the Mendicant orders), and, at the same time, professor of divinity in the university which had been erected at Wittenberg a few years before this period by Fredric the Wise," Mosheim, Vol, 2, See. 1, Chapter 2, See, 1.

3—Z
"The reformed religion was propagated in Sweden, soon after Luther's rupture with Rome, by one of his disciples whose name was Claus Petri, and who was the first lie raider of religious liberty in that kingdom. The zealous efforts of this missionary were powerfully seconded by that valiant and public-spirited prince, Gustavus Vasa Ericson, whom the Swedes had raised to the throne in the place of Christiern, king of Denmark, whose horrid barbarity lost him the scepter that he had perfidiously usurped." Mosheim, V. 2, See. 1, Chap. 2, Sec. 30. Britannica, V. 22, p. 754, Article—Sweden,

4—A
"The light of the reformation was also received in Denmark, in consequence of the ardent desire discovered by Christian or Christiean II, of having his subjects instructed in the principles and doctrines of Luther. This monarch whose savage and infernal cruelty rendered his name odious and his memory execrable, was nevertheless desirous of delivering his dominions from the superstition and tyranny of Rome. It is, however, proper to observe that in all these proceedings, Christiern was animated by no other motive than that of ambition. . . . A revolution produced by his

avarice, tyranny, and cruelty, prevented the execution of this bold enterprise. 'The states of the kingdom, being exasperated, some by his schemes for the destroying the liberty of Denmark, others by his attempts to abolish the superstition of their ancestors. . . . formed a conspiracy against him in 1523 by which he was deposed and banished from his dominions, and his uncle, Fredric, duke of Holstein, placed on the Danish throne." Mosheim, V. 2, Sec. 1, Chap. 2, Sec. 31.

4—B
"Predestinarian Baptists: This body exists mostly in the Southwest of the United States. Their name denotes that they hold to the seed of death implanted in man by his fall from primitive holiness, the fruit of which is death, and the seed of life implanted by the Holy Ghost, the fruit of which is eternal life. They hold with vigor to the five points of Calvinism." Britannica, V. 25, p. 355. Article—Baptists

4—C
"The initial conditions of Scottish Presbyterianism are seen in the historical facts—(1) that the Reformation was the form taken by the triumph of a violent and grasping aristocracy over the encroachments of the sovereign and an alien church; and (2) that John Knox was its spiritual leader. Under his advice the Protestant nobles in December, 1557, formed themselves into a covenanted body called "The Lords of the Congregation;" in 1559 Perth declared itself Protestant, and Knox's sermon there on the 11th of May, was the manifesto of revolt." Britannica, V. 19, p. 679. Article—Presbyterianism. Mosheim, V. 2, p. 112.

4—D
"The founder of the Reformed Church was Ulrich Zwingli, a native of Switzerland, and a man of uncommon penetration and acuteness, accompanied with an ardent zeal for truth. This great man was for removing out of the churches, and abolishing, in the ceremonies and appendages of public worship, many things

which Luther was disposed to treat with toleration and indulgence, such as images, altars, wax tapers, the form of exorcism, and private confession." Mosheim, V. 2, p. 104, Chapter 2, Section 3.

4—E
"The sect of Quakers received this denomination in the year 1650, from Gervas Bennet, a justice of peace in Derbyshire, partly on account of the convulsive agitations and shakings of the body with which their discourses to the people were usually attended, and partly on account of the exhortation addressed to this magistrate by Fox and his companions, who, when they were called before him, desired him, with a loud voice and a vehement emotion of the body to tremble at the word of the Lord." However, sarcastic this appellation may be, when considered in its origin in the members of this sect are willing to adopt it, provided it be rightly understood; they prefer, nevertheless, to be called, in allusion to that doctrine which is the fundamental principle of their association, "Children or confessors of Light. In their conversation and intercourse with each other, they use no other term of appellation than that of Friend. This seed had its rise in England in those unhappy times of confusion, anarchy, and civil discord, when every political or religious fanatic had formed a new plan of government, or invented a new system of theology, came forth with his novelties to public view, and propagated them with impunity among a fickle and unthinking multitude. Its parent or founder was George Pox, a shoemaker of a dark and melancholy complexion, and of a visionary and enthusiastic turn of mind. About the year 1647, which was the 24th year of his age, he began to stroll through several counties of England, giving himself out for a person divinely inspired, and exhorting the people to attend to the voice of the divine word, that lies hidden in the hearts of all men." Mosheim, V. 2, Chap. 4, See. 1. Hist, of Quakers. Britannica, V. 9, Article—Fox. See also 9—G.

30 | *Historical Quotations*

4—F
"In a word, Brown endeavored to model the form of the church after the infant community that was founded by the apostles. . . The sect of this hot-headed innovator, not being able to endure the severe treatment which their opposition to the established forms of religious government and worship had drawn upon them, . . . retired into the Netherlands Their founder returned into England, and having renounced his principles of separation, took orders in the established church, and obtained a benefice. The Puritan exiles, whom he thus abandoned, disagreed among themselves, and split into parties; and their affairs declined from day to day. This engaged the wiser part of them to mitigate the severity of their founder's plan, and to soften the rigor of his uncharitable decisions; and hence arose the community of the Independents or Congregational Brethren." Mosheim, V. 2, Chap. 2, See. 21. Hist. Reformed Ch. Britannica, V. 4, Article—Brownists. p. 392.

4—G
"DUNKERS or TUNKERS, a sect of American Baptists originating in Germany. The name, as its second form indicates, is a nickname meaning dippers, from the German tunken, to dip. From the first the members recognized no other name than 'Brethren.' The founder of the sect was Alexander Mack of Schwartzenau, who, along with one or two companions, was led to adopt anti-pedobaptist views about the year 1708. It had scarcely assumed organized existence in Germany when its members were compelled by persecutions to take refuge in Holland, from which they emigrated to Pennsylvania between 1720 and 1929." Britannica, V. 7, Page 543, Article—Dunkers.

4—H
"The year 1528 may justly be fixed as the turning point or Henry's (the 8th) life. By that time the divorce had become a national and even a European question, and Henry had decisively committed himself to the course which was to result in the separation

from Borne. . . . Soon after the king took a step which precipitated the crisis; he married Anne Boleyn, an event which w.as quickly followed by the publication in Flanders of a threat of excommunication from Borne. After this, the act of appeals was passed, forbidding appeals from the English ecclesiastical courts to Borne, and Cranmer, in a court at Dunstable, declared the marriage with Catherine null and void. In the following year (1534) the papal authority in England was annulled, and by the Act of Supremacy Henry was declared supreme head of the English Church." Britannica, V. 11, Page 664, Article—Henry VIII. Mosheim, V, 2, Chap. 3, Sec. II Hist, of Reformation.

4—I
"This degeneracy was observed with sensations of horror by John and Charles Wesley, who were then students at the University of Oxford, and had contracted a serious turn of mind from the writings of William Law, the celebrated mystic. These devout brothers passed a great part of their time in religious conversation, in reflecting on the interesting contents of the Holy Scriptures, and in private prayer. They were joined by some other academies who were religiously disposed; and a sect which afterward made an extraordinary progress, took its rise in the year 1729, deriving the appellation of METHODISTS from the regular distribution of their time, their orderly and composed demeanor, and the supposed purity of their religious principles." Mosheim, V. 2, p. 393, Chap. 4, Hist. Ch. England. Britannica, V. 24, p. 504, Article—Wesley. Methodist Discipline: "Historical Statement."

4—J
"The churches, in those early days, were entirely independent, none of them being subject to any foreign jurisdiction, but each governed by its own rulers and its own laws; for, though the churches founded by the apostles had this particular deference shown to them, that they were consulted in difficult and doubtful cases, yet they had no juridical authority, no sort of supremacy over the others, nor the least right to enact law's for them. Noth-

ing, on the contrary, is more evident than the perfect equality that reigned among the primitive churches, nor does there ever appear, in this first century, the smallest trace of that association of provincial churches, from which councils and metropolitans derive their origin. It was only in the 2nd century that the custom of holding council commenced in Greece, whence it soon spread through the other provinces." Mosheim, Cen. 1, Part 2, Chap. 2, Section 14.

4—K
"Let none, however, confound the bishop of this primitive and golden period of the church with those of whom we read in the following ages; for, though they were both distinguished by the same name, yet they differed in many respects. A bishop during the first and second century, was a person who had the care of one Christian assembly, which, at that time was, generally speaking, small enough to be contained in a private house. In this assembly he acted, not so much with the authority of a master, as with the zeal and diligence of a faithful servant. He instructed the people, performed the several parts of divine worship, attended the sick, and inspected the circumstances and supplies of the poor. He charged, indeed, the presbyters with the performance of those duties and services, which the multiplicity, of his engagements rendered it impossible for him to fulfill; but he had not the power to decide or enact anything without the consent of the presbyters and people. And, though the episcopal office was. both laborious and singularly dangerous, yet its revenues were very small, since the church had no certain income, but depended on the gifts or oblations of the multitude, which were, no doubt, inconsiderable, and were moreover to be divided among the bishops, presbyters, deacons, and poor," Mosheim, Cen. 1, Part 2, Chap. 2, Section 12. Gibbon, chap. 15, between notes 107, 108.

4—L
"The power and jurisdiction of the bishops were not long confined to these narrow limits, but were soon extended by the fol-

lowing means. The bishops, who lived in the cities, had, either by their own ministry, or that of their presbyters, erected new churches in the neighboring towns and villages. These churches, continuing under the inspection and ministry of the bishops, by whose labors and counsels they had engaged to embrace the Gospel, grew imperceptibly into ecclesiastical provinces which the Greeks afterwards called dioceses. But, as the bishop of the city could not extend his labors and inspection to all these churches in the country and in the villages, he appointed certain suffragans or deputies to govern and instruct these new societies; and they were distinguished by the title of Chorepiscopi, i. e. country bishops. This order held the middle rank between bishops and presbyters." Mosheim, Cen. 1, Part 2, Chap. 2, Sec. 13.

4—M
"During a great part of this (2nd) century, the Christian churches were independent with respect to each other; nor were they joined by association, confederacy, or any other bonds than those of charity. Each Christian assembly was a little state, governed by its own laws, which were either enacted, or at least, approved by the society. But in process of time, all the Christian churches of a province were formed into one large ecclesiastical body, which, like confederate states assembled at a certain time in order to deliberate about the common interests of the whole. This institution had its origin among the Greeks with whom nothing was more common than this confederacy of independent states, and the regular assemblies which met, in consequence thereof, at fixed times, and were composed of the deputies of each respective state. But these ecclesiastical associations were not long confined to the Greeks; their great utility was no sooner perceived, than they became universal, and were formed in all places where the Gospel had been planted. To these assemblies, in which the deputies or commissioners of several churches consulted together, the names of synods was appropriated by the Greeks, and that of councils by the Latins; and the laws that were enacted in these general meetings, were called canons, i. e. rules." Mosheim, Cen.

2, Part 2, Chap. 2, Sec. 2. Neander, p. 119; Jones' Church History, Chapter 3, Sec. 1.

4—N
"These councils, of which we find not the smallest trace before the middle of this (2nd) century, changed the whole face of the church, and gave it a new form; for by them the ancient privileges of the people were considerably diminished, and the power and the authority of the bishops greatly augmented." Neander, page 120. Mosheim, Cen. 2, Part 2, Chap. 2, Sec. 3.

4—O
"The face of things began now to change in the Christian church. The ancient method of ecclesiastical government seemed, in general, still to subsist, while at the same time, by imperceptible steps, it varied from the primitive rule, and degenerated toward the form of a religious monarchy; for the bishops aspired to higher degrees of power and authority than they formerly possessed, and not only violated the rights of the people, but also made gradual encroachments upon the privileges of the presbyters." Mosheim, Cen. 3, Part. 2, Chap. 2, Sec. 3.

4—P
"Hence, at the conclusion of this (4th) century, there remained no more than a mere shadow of the ancient government at the church. Many of the privileges which had belonged to the presbyters and people were usurped by the bishops; and many of the rights, which had been formerly vested in the universal church, were transferred to the emperors and to subordinate officers and magistrates." Mosheim, Cen. 4, Part 2, Chap. 2, Sec. 2.

4—Q
"Constantine, in order to prevent civil commotions, and to fix his authority upon solid and stable foundations, made several changes, not only in the laws of the empire, but also in the form of the Roman government; and as there were many important

reasons, which induced him to suit the administration of the church to these changes in the civil constitution, this necessarily introduced, among the bishops, new degrees of eminence and rank. Three prelates had, before this enjoyed a certain degree of pre-eminence over the rest of the episcopal order, viz. the bishops of Rome, Antioch, and Alexandria; and to these the bishop of Constantinople was added when the imperial residence was transferred to that city. These four prelates answered to the four Praetorian prefects created by Constantine; and it is possible that, in this very century, they were distinguished by the Jewish title of patriarchs." Mosheim, Cen. 4, Part 2, Chap. 2, See. 3.

4—R
"Encouraged by this (the high rank of Jerusalem) and animated by the favor and protection of the younger Theodosious, the aspiring prelate, (Juvenal, bishop of Jerusalem) not only assumed the dignity of patriarch of all Palestine, a rank that rendered him supreme and independent of all spiritual authority, but also invaded the rights of the bishop of Antioch, and usurped his jurisdiction over the provinces of Phoenicia and Arabia. Henee arose a warm contest between Juvenal and Maximus, bishop of Antioch, which the council of Chalcedon decided by restoring to the latter the provinces of Phoenicia and Arabia, and confirming the former in the spiritual possession of all Palestine, and in the high rank which he had assumed in the church. Thus were created, in the fifth century, five superior rulers of the church, who were distinguished from the rest by the title PATRIARCHS." Mosheim, Ceu. 5, Part 1, Chap. 2, See. 2.

4—S
"If, indeed, we are to give credit to Anastasius and Paul the Deacon, something like what we have now related was transacted by Phocas; for, when the bishops of Constantinople maintained that their church was not only equal in dignity and authority to that of Rome, but also the head of all the Christian churches, this tyrant opposed their pretensions, and granted the pre-eminence to the

church of Rome: and thus was the papal supremacy first introduced." Mosheim, Cen. 7, Part 2, Chap. 2, Sec. 1.

4—T
"This prodigious accession to the opulence and authority of the clergy in the west 'began with their head, the Roman Pontiff, and spread gradually from him among the inferior bishops, and also among the sacerdotal and monastic orders. The barbarous nations, who received the Gospel, looked upon the bishop of Rome as the successor of their chief Druid, or high priest. And as this tremendous druid had enjoyed, under the darkness of paganism, a boundless authority, and had been treated with a degree of veneration, that, through its servile excess, degenerated into terror; so the barbarous nations on their conversion to Christianity, thought proper to confer upon the chief of the bishops the same honors and the same authority that had formerly been vested in their arch-druid. The pope received, with something more than a mere spiritual delight, these august privileges; and lest, upon any change of affairs, attempts might be made to deprive him of them, he strengthened his title to these extraordinary honors, by a variety of passages drawn from ancient history, and (what was still more astonishing) by arguments of a religious nature. This conduct of a superstitious people swelled the arrogance of the Roman-druid to an enormous size, and gave to the see of Rome, in civil and political affairs, a high pre-eminence and a despotic authority, unknown in former ages. Hence, among other unhappy circumstances, arose that monstrous and most pernicious opinion, that such persons as were excluded from the communion of the church by the pontiff himself, or any of the bishops, forfeited thereby not only their civil rights and advantages as citizens, but even the common claims and privileges of humanity. This horrid opinion, which was a fatal source of wars, massacres, and rebellions without number, and which contributed more than, any other means to augment and confirm the papal authority, was, unhappily for Europe, borrowed by Christians, or rather by the

clergy, from the pagan superstitions." Mosheim, Cen. 8, Part 2, Chap. 2, See. 6.

4—U
"The supreme dominion, over the church and its possessions, was vested in the emperors and kings, both in the eastern and the western world. . . . No decrees of any council obtained the force of laws, until they were approved and confirmed by the supreme magistrate. Thus was the spiritual authority of Rome wisely bound by the civil." Mosheim, Cen. 8, Part 2, Chap. 2, Sec. 15, 16.

4—V
"The authority and luster of the Latin church, or, to speak more properly, the power and dominion of the Roman pontiffs, rose in this century to the highest point, though they rose by degrees, and had much opposition and many difficulties to conquer." Mosheim, Cen. 11, Part 2, Chap. 2, See. 2.

4—W
"Here (at the residence of the pope) the suppliant prince (Henry) unmindful of his dignity, stood, during three days, in the open air at the entrance of this fortress with his feet bare, his head uncovered. . . . on the 4th day he was admitted to the presence of the lordly pontiff, who with difficulty granted him the absolution he demanded; . . . forbidding him, at the same time, to assume, during this interval, the title of king." Mosheim, Cen. 11, Part 2, Chap. 2, Sec. 16.

4—X
"After the defeat of Licinius, the empire was ruled by Constantine alone until his death; and the Christian cause experienced, in its happy progress, the effects of his auspicious administration. This zealous prince employed all the resources of his genius, all the authority of his laws, and all the engaging charms of his munificence and liberality, to efface, by degrees, the superstitions of

paganism, and to propagate Christianity in every corner of the Roman Empire." Mosheim, Cen. 4, Part 1, Chap. 1, See. 10.

4—Y
"Constantine the Great made no essential alteration in the form of government that took place in the Christian church before his time; he only corrected it in some particulars, and gave it a greater extent. Although he permitted the church to remain a body-politic, distinct from that of the state, as it had formerly been, yet he assumed to himself the supreme power over this sacred body, and the right of modeling and governing it in such a manner as should be most conducive to the public good. This right he enjoyed without opposition. The ecclesiastical laws were enacted, either by the emperor (State) or by councils (Church)." Mosheim, Cen. 4, Part 2, Chap. 2, Sec. 1 and 6.

4—Z
"And as there were many important reasons, which induced him (Constantine) to suit the administration of the church to these changes in the civil constitution, this necessarily introduced, among the bishops, new degrees of eminence and rank." Mosheim, Cen. 4, Part 2, Chap. 2, Sec. 3.

5—A
"The place of his (Christ's) birth was Bethlehem, in Palestine. The year in which it happened, has not hitherto been ascertained, notwithstanding the deep and laborious researches of the learned. There is nothing surprising in this, when we consider that the first Christians labored under the same difficulties, and were divided in their opinions concerning the time of Christ's birth. That which appears most probable, is, that it happened about a year and six months before the death of Herod, in the year of Borne 748 or 740. The uncertainty however, of this point, is of no great consequence. We know that the Son of Righteousness has shined upon the world; and though we cannot fix the precise period in which He arose, this will not preclude us from enjoying the direc-

tion and influence of His vital and salutary beams." Mosheim, Cen. 1, Part 1, Chap. 3, See. 1. Neander, page 191. Eusebius Ch. Hist. B, 1. Ch 5 and note.

5—B
"The consequences of this wretched theology were a universal corruption and depravity of manners, which appeared in the impunity of the most flagitious crimes. Juvenal and Persius among the Latins, and Lucian among the Greeks, bear testimony to the justice of this heavy accusation. It is also well known, that no public law prohibited the sports of the gladiators, the exercise of unnatural lusts, the licentiousness of divorce, the custom of exposing infants; and of procuring abortions, or the frontless atrocity of publicly consecrating stews and brothels to certain divinities." Mosheim, Cen. 1, Part 1, Chap. 1, Sec. 14.

5—C
"A new method also of proceeding with penitents was introduced into the Latin church; for grievous offenders, who had formerly been obliged to confess their guilt in the face of the congregation, were now delivered from this mortifying penalty, and obtained, from Leo the Great, a permission to confess their crimes privately to a priest appointed for that purpose. By this change of the ancient discipline, one of the greatest restraints upon licentiousness, (and the only remaining barrier of chastity) was entirely removed, and the actions of Christians were subject to no other scrutiny than that of the clergy; a change which was frequently convenient for the sinner, and also advantageous in many respects to the sacred order." Mosheim, Cen. 5, Part 2, Chap. 4, Sec. 3.

5—D
"The first day of the week, which was the ordinary and stated time for the public assemblies of Christians, was in consequence of a peculiar law enacted by Constantine, observed with greater solemnity than it had formerly been."

Mosheim, Cen. 4, Part 2, Chap. 4, See. 5.
Gibbon, Decline, Vol. 2, Page 163.
Fisher, History of the Christian Church, Page 118.
Eusebius, Life of Constantine, B 4, G 18.

5—E

"All Christians were unanimous in setting apart the first day of the week on which the triumphant Saviour arose from the dead, for the solemn celebration of public worship."

Mosheim, Cen. 1, Part 2, Chap. 4, See. 4.
Britannica, Vol. 22, P. 654, Quotation from Justin. Art. Sunday.
Fisher, History of the Christian Church, Page 40.
Gibbon, Chapter 20.

5—F

The first female convent known in the Christian world was instituted by Louis I, Emperor of Borne in the ninth century, Mosheim, Cen. 9, Part 2, Chap. 2, Sec. 12.

5—G

"Now, Comparative Philology does present to us cases where there is reason to presume an original participation in a high civilization, though the present condition of the race is almost the lowest conceivable. An instance of this kind is furnished by the very curious race still existing in Ceylon, and known as the 'Weddas.' The best comparative philologists pronounce the language of the Weddas to be a debase descendant of the most elaborate and earliest known form of Aryan speech—the Sanskrit; and the Weddas are on this ground believed to be degenerate descendants of the Sanskritic Aryans who conquered India. If this be indeed so, it is difficult to conceive of a degeneration which could be more complete. The Sanskritic Aryans must, by their language and literature, have been at the time of their conquest, in a fairly advanced stage of civilization. The Weddas are savages of a type than which it is scarcely possible to conceive anything more debased. Their language is limited to some few hundred vocables; they cannot count beyond two or three; they have, of course, no idea of letters; they have domesticated no animal but the dog; they have no arts beyond the power of making bows and, arrows and constructing huts of a very rude kind; they are said to have no idea of God, and scarcely any memory. They with difficulty obtain a subsistence by means of the bow, and are continually dwindling, and threaten to become extinct. In height they rarely exceed five feet, and are thus degenerate both physically and mentally. " Rawlinson, The Origin of Nations, pp. 6 and 7.

5—H
"These views all claim to be the results of original research, and have been put forward by persons (more or less) acquainted with the Egyptian monuments, and (more or less) competent to translate and expound the hierographical inscriptions. Before proceeding to explain how it comes to be possible that such different views can be taken, it will, perhaps help the reader to appreciate the diversity if we tabulate the views themselves, and express numerically their differences.

DATE FOR ACCESSION OF MENES

	B. C.
Mariette and Lenormant	5004
Brugseh	4400
Lepsius	3892
Bunsen (early view)	3623
Bunsen (later view)	3059
Stuart Poole	2717
G. Wilkinson	2691

Rawlinson, The Origin of Nations, p. 21.

5—I
"Such are the chronological views which profane history, monumental and other, studied by itself, seems to us on the whole to

favor. We should maintain them had the Bible never been written, or had it been entirely devoid of all chronological notices. But we think it right to call the attention of our readers, whom we presume to be believers in revelation, to the fact that these views, while irreconcilable with the wholly unauthorized chronology of Archbishop Usher, harmonize admirably with the Biblical numbers, as they are given in the version called the Septuagint."

We subjoin a tabular view of the chief chronological conclusions at which we have arrived in the course of this inquiry:

	(about) B. C.
Date of Deluge, according to Septuagint	3200
Rise of monarchy in Egypt	(probably) 2450
Rise of monarch in Babylon	(probably) 2300
Earliest traces of civilization in Asia Minor	(probably) 2000
Rise of Phoenicia	1550
Rise of Assyria	1500
Earliest Iranic civilization (Zandavesta)	1500
Earliest Indic civilization (vedas)	1200
Earliest Hellenic civilization (Homer)	1200
Phrygian and Lydian civilization commerce	900
Etruscan civilization commences	650
Lyeian civilization commences	600

Rawlinson—The Origin of Nations, pp. 160, 161,

5—J

"The account which Berosus gives of the Deluge is still more strikingly in accordance with the narrative of Scripture, 'Xisuthrus,' he says, 'was warned by Saturn in a dream that all mankind would be destroyed shortly by a deluge of rain. He was bidden to bury in the city of Zippara (or Sepharvaim) such written documents as existed; and then to build a huge vessel or ark, in length five furlongs, and two furlongs in width, wherein was to be placed good store of provisions, together with winged fowl and four-footed beasts of the earth; and in which he was himself to embark with his wife and children, and his close friends. Xisuthrus did accordingly, and the flood came the time appointed. The ark drifted towards Armenia; and Xisuthrus, on the third day after the rain abated, sent out from the ark a bird, which, after flying for a while over the illimitable sea of waters, and finding neither food nor a spot on which it could settle, returned to him. Some days later Xisuthrus sent out other birds, which likewise returned, but with feet covered with mud. Sent out a third time, the birds returned no more; and Xisuthrus knew that the earth had reappeared. So, he removed some of the covering of the ark, and looked, and behold the vessel had grounded upon a high mountain and remained fixed. Then he went forth from the ark, with his wife, his daughter, and his pilot, and built an altar, and offered sacrifice; after which he suddenly disappeared from sight together with those who had accompanied him. They who had remained in the ark, surprised that he did not return, sought him: and when they heard his voice in the sky, exhorting them to continue religious, and bidding them go back to Babylonia from the land of Armenia, where they were, and recover the buried documents, and make them once more known among men. So they obeyed, and went back to the land of Babylon, and built many cities and temples, and raised up Babylon from its ruins." Rawlinson—Historical Evidences, p. 67.

5—K
"At this time the ancient race of men were so puffed up with their strength and tallness of stature, that they began to despise and condemn the gods; and labored to erect that very lofty tower, which is now called Babylon, intending thereby to scale heaven. But when the building approached the sky, behold, the gods called in the aid of the winds, and by their help overturned the tower and cast it to the ground. The name of the ruins is still called Babel; because until this time all men had used the same speech, but now there was sent upon them a confusion of many and divers tongues." Rawlinson—Historical Evidences, p. 70. (Quotation based upon Berosus, a heathen writer)

5—L
"The age was an historical age, (not mythological) being that of Dionysius, Diodorus, Livy, Velleius, Paterculus, Plutarch, Valerius Maximus, and Tacitus—the country was one where written records were kept, and historical literature had long flourished; it produced at the very time when the New Testament documents were being written, an historian of good repute, Josephus, whose narrative of the events of his own time is universally -accepted as authentic and trustworthy. To suppose that a mythology could be formed in such an age and such a country, is to confuse the characteristics of the most opposite periods—to ascribe to a time of luxury, over-civilization, and decay, a phase of thought which only belongs to the rude vigor and early infancy of nations." Rawlinson, Historical Evidences, p. 175.

5—M
Pliny writes to Trajan, "It is my custom, sir, to refer to you all things about which I am in doubt. For who is more capable of directing my hesitancy, or instructing my ignorance? I have never been present at any trials of the Christians; consequently, I do not know what is the nature of their crimes, or the usual strictness of their examination, or severity of their punishment. I have moreover hesitated not a little, whether any distinction was to be made in respect to age, or whether those of tender years were to be treated the same as adults; whether repentance entitles them to a pardon, or whether it shall avail nothing for him who has once been a Christian to renounce his error; whether the name itself, even without any crime, should subject him to punishment, or only the crimes connected with the name. In the meantime, I have perused this course toward those who have been brought before me as Christians, I asked them whether they were Christians; if they confessed, I repeated the question a second and a third time, adding threats of punishments. If they still persevered, I ordered them to be led away to punishment; for I could not doubt, whatever the nature of their profession might be, that a stubborn and unyielding obstinacy certainly deserved to be punished. There

were others also under the like infatuation; but as they were Roman citizens, I directed them to be sent to the capitol. But the crime spread, as is wont to happen, even while the persecutions were going on, and numerous instances presented themselves. An information was presented to me without any name subscribed, accusing a large number of persons, who denied that they were Christians, or had ever been. They repeated after me an invocation of the gods, and made offerings with frankincense and wine before your statue, which I had ordered to be brought for this purpose, together with the image of the gods; and moreover they reviled Christ; whereas those who are truly Christians, it is said, cannot be forced to do any of these things. I thought, therefore, that they ought to be discharged. Others, who were accused by a witness, confessed that they were Christians but said that they had renounced their error, some three years before, others more, and a few even as many as twenty years ago. They all did homage to your statue and the images of the gods, and at the same time reviled the name of Christ. They declared that the whole of their guilt or error was, that they were accustomed to meet on a stated day before it was light, and to sing, in concert a hymn of praise to Christ, as God, and to bind themselves by an oath not for the perpetration of any wickedness, but that they would not commit any theft, robbery, or adultery, nor violate their word, nor refuse, when called upon, to restore anything committed to their trust. After this they were accustomed to separate, and then to reassemble to eat in common a harmless meal. Even this, however, they ceased to do, after my edict, in which, agreeably to your commands, I forbade the meeting of secret assemblies. After hearing this, I thought it the more necessary to endeavor to find out the truth by putting to the torture two female slaves who were called 'deaconesses.' But I could discover nothing but a perverse and extravagant superstition; and therefore I deferred all further proceedings until I should consult with you. For the matter appears to me worthy of such consultation, especially on account of the number of those who are involved in peril. For many of every age, of, every rank, and either sex, are exposed and will be exposed to danger. Nor has the contagion of this superstition been confined to the cities only but it has extended to the villages, and even to the country. Nevertheless, it still seems possible to arrest the evil, and to apply a remedy. At least it is very evident, that the temples, which had already been almost deserted, begin to be frequented, and the sacred solemnities, so long interrupted, are again revived; and the victims, which heretofore could hardly find a purchaser, are now every where in demand. From this it is easy to image what a multitude of men might be reclaimed, if pardon should be offered to those who repent."

Trajan replies, "You have pursued the right course, my dear Pliny, in conducting the case of those Christians who were brought before you. Nor is it possible to adopt one uniform and invariable mode of proceeding. I would not have you seek out these persons; if they are brought before you, and are convicted, they must be punished; yet with this privos, that he who denies that he is a Christian, and confirms his denial by naturally invoking our gods, however he may have been suspected in the past, shall obtain pardon upon his repentance. But information without the accuser's name subscribed, ought not to be received in prosecutions of any kind; for they are of the worst tendency, and are unworthy of the age in which we live." (PLINY-Epist., X. 97, 98.) Quoted by Rawlinson—Historical Evidences, pp 384-386.

5—N

"The titles which the books bear in the modern authorized versions of the Scriptures are literal translations from some of the most ancient Greek manuscripts and descend to us at least from the times of the first Councils; while titles still more emphatic and explicit are found in several of the versions which were made at an early period. . . . Headings, it must be remembered, are in no case any part of the inspired Word; they indicate merely the option of those who had the custody of the Word at the time when they were prefixed. Now in most eases the headings would be attached soon after the composition of the work, when its authorship was certainly known." Rawlinson—Historical Evidence, p. 159-160. See also Horne's Introduction, Vol. 1, p. 215.

5—O
"But out of all this confusion and uncertainty a very small and simple discovery made a few years since has educed order and harmony in a very remarkable way. It is found that Nabonadius, the last king of the Canon, associated with him on the throne during the later years of his reign his son, Bil-shar-uzar, (Belshazzar) and allowed him the royal title. There can be little doubt that it was this prince who conducted the defense of Babylon, and was slain in the massacre which followed the capture; while his father, who was at the time in Borsippa, surrendered, and experienced the clemency which was generally shown to fallen kings by the Persians. . . . My attention has been further drawn to a very remarkable illustration which the discovery of Belshazzar's position as joint ruler with his father furnishes to an expression twice repeated in Daniel, fifth chapter. The promise made and performed to Daniel is, that he shall be the third ruler in the kingdom. Formerly it was impossible to explain this, or to understand why he was not the second ruler, as he seems to have been under Nebuchadnezzar, and as Joseph was in Egypt, and Mordecai in Persia. It now appears, that, as there were two kings at the same time, Belshazzar, in subject, could only make him the third personage in the Empire." Rawlinson, Historical Evidences, pp. 139, 442.

5—P
"The only instance in which the avowed rejectors of revelation have possessed the supreme power and government of a country, and have attempted to dispose of human happiness according to their own doctrines and wishes, is that of France during the greater part of the revolution, which, it is now well known, was effected by the abettors of infidelity. The great majority of the nation had become infidels. The name and profession of Christianity was renounced by the legislature, and the abolition of the

Christian era was proclaimed. Death was declared by an act of the republican government to be an eternal sleep. The existence of the Deity, and the immortality of the soul, were formally disavowed by the National Convention; and the doctrine of the resurrection from the dead was declared to have been only preached by superstition for the torment of the living. All the religions in the world were proclaimed to be the daughters of ignorance and pride; and it was decreed to be the duty of the convention to assume the honorable office of disseminating atheism (which was blasphemously affirmed to be truth) over all the world. As a part of this duty, the convention further decreed, that its express renunciation of all religious worship should, like its invitations to rebellion, be translated into all foreign languages; and it was asserted and received in the convention, that the adversaries of religion had deserved well of their country. Correspondent with these professions and declarations were the effects actually produced. Public worship was utterly abolished. The churches were converted into 'temples of reason,' in which atheistical and licentious homilies were substituted for the prescribed service; and an absurd and ludicrous imitation of the pagan mythology was exhibited under the title of the 'religion of reason.' In the principal church of every town a tutelary goddess was installed with a ceremony equally pedantic, frivolous, and profane and the females, selected to personify this new divinity were mostly prostitutes, who received the adoration of the attendant municipal officers, and of the multitudes whom fear, or force, or motive of gain, had collected together on the occasion. Contempt for religion or decency became the test of attachment to the government; and the gross infraction of any moral or social duty was deemed a proof of civism, and a victory over prejudice. All distinctions of right and wrong were eon- founded. The grossest debauchery triumphed. The reign of atheism and of reason was the reign of terror." HORNE'S INTRODUCTION, Vol. 1, Page 25.

5—Q

"On all these subjects," says Michaelis, "is thrown the fullest light, as soon as we examine the special history of that period; a light which is not confined to the present, but extends itself to the following chapters, insomuch that it cannot be doubted that this book (Acts of Apostles) was written, not after the destruction of Jerusalem, but by a person who was contemporary to the events which are there related. Ananias, the son of Nebedeni, was high priest at the time that Helena, Queen of Abilene, supplied the Jews with corn from Egypt, during the famine which took place in the fourth year of Claudious, mentioned in the eleventh chapter of the Acts. St. Paul, therefore, who took a journey to Jerusalem at that period, could not have been ignorant of the elevation of Ananias to that dignity. Soon after the holding of the first council, as it is called, at Jerusalem, Ananias was dispossessed of his office, in consequence of certain acts of violence between the Samaritans and the Jews, and sent prisoner to Rome, whence he was afterward released, and returned to Jerusalem. Now from that period he could not be called high-priest in the proper sense of the word, though Josephus has sometimes given him the title of ARXIEREUS taken in the more extensive meaning of a priest, who had a seat and voice in the Sanhedrin; and Jonathan, though we are not acquainted with the circumstances of his elevation, had been raised in the meantime to the supreme dignity of the Jewish church. Between the death of Jonathan, who was murdered by order of Felix, and the high-priest-hood of Ishmael, who was invested with that office by Agrippa, elapsed an interval in which this dignity continued vacant. Now it happened precisely in this interval that St. Paul was apprehended in Jerusalem; and the Sanhedrin being destitute of a president, he undertook of his own authority the discharge of that office, which he executed with the greatest tyranny. It is possible, therefore that St. Paul who had been only a few days in Jerusalem, might be ignorant that Ananias, who had been dispossessed of the priest-hood, had taken upon himself a trust to which he was not entitled; he might therefore very naturally exclaim, 'I wist not, brethren, that he was the high-priest! Admitting him, on the other hand, to have been acquainted with the fact, the expression must, be considered as an indirect reproof, and a tacit refusal to recognize usurped authority. A passage, then, which has hitherto been involved in obscurity, is brought by this relation into the Clearest light; and the whole history of St. Paul's imprisonment, the conspiracy of the fifty Jews with the consent of the Sanhedrin, their petition to Festus to send him to Caesarea, with intent to murder him on the road, are facts which correspond to the character of the times as described by Josephus who mentions the principal persons recorded in the Acts, and paints their profligacy in colors even stronger than those of St, Luke." Quoted by HORNE, Vol. 1, p. 50. Jones Ch. Hist. V. 1, p. 73.

5—R
"But now Pilate, the procurator of Judea, removed the army from Caesarea to Jerusalem, to take their winter quarters there, in order to abolish the Jewish laws. So, he introduced Caesar's effigies, which were upon the ensigns, and brought them into the city; whereas our law forbids us the very making of images; on which account the former procurators were wont to make their entry into the city with such ensigns as had not those ornaments. Pilate was the first who brought those images to Jerusalem, and set them up there; which was done without the knowledge of the people, because it was done in the night-time; but as soon as they knew it, they came in multitudes to Caesarea, and interceded with Pilate many days, that he would remove the images; and when he would not grant their requests, because it would tend to the injury of Caesar, while yet they persevered in their request, on the sixth day he ordered his soldiers to have their weapons privately, while he came and sat upon his judgment seat, which seat was so prepared in open place of the city, that it concealed the army that lay ready to oppress them. And when the Jews petitioned him again, he gave a signal to the soldiers to encompass them round, and threatened that their punishment should be no less than immediate death unless they would leave off disturbing

him, and go their ways home. But they threw themselves upon the ground, and laid their necks bare, and said they would take their death very willingly, rather than the wisdom of their laws should be transgressed; upon which Pilate was deeply affected with their firm resolution to keep their laws inviolable, and presently commanded the images to be carried back from Jerusalem to Caesarea." Josephus, Ant. 18-3-1.

"The captivity, though a judgment on the people for their sins of unfaithfulness to the covenant, was in reality an unconscious preparation for the times of the Messiah. 'Their national loss was turned to gain; not only were they weaned from their proneness to idolatry, but their departures from monotheism were, after meeting with Persian types of thought, corrected and reformed . . . . The return from captivity is thus the third and final stage in the growth of Israel as the covenant people. Monotheism, exceptional in the days of Elijah and the early prophets, was burned into them by the fires of persecution. This highest stage of monotheism was the elevated point of view which they had reached in the third and final stage of their spiritual growth on the return from captivity." J. B. Heard, Lecturer, University of Cambridge. Page 68 in "Bible Helps," International. Prideaux, Ano. 167.

5—S

From the following quotation, it is easily seen why the armies of Babylonia and the Mesopotamian lands in general, when they wished to get into the region of Palestine, would descend into that country from the "north." "Extending for above two hundred miles from north to south, (that is, from near Mt. Amanus to the hills of Galilee) almost in a direct line, and without further break than an occasional screen of low hills, it furnishes the most convenient line of passage between Asia and Africa, alike for the journeys of merchants and for the march of armies. Along this line passed Thothmes and Ramases, Sargon and Sennacherib, Necho and Nebuchadnezzar, Alexander and his war-like successors, Pompey, Anthony, Kaled, Godfrey of Bouillon; along this must pass every great army which, starting from the general seats of power in Western Asia, seeks conquests in Africa, or which, proceeding from Africa, aims at the acquisition of an Asiatic dominion." Rawlinson's Ancient Monarchies, V. 2, p. 443; Rawlinson's History of Egypt, V. 1, p. 21.

5—T
"With the cities of Phoenicia and the fleets of the Mediterranean subject to his control, Alexander easily effected the reduction of Egypt . . . . Altogether the Ptolemies reigned in Egypt almost exactly three centuries. The rulers who held the throne for the last two hundred years or more, with few exceptions, were a succession of monsters, such as ever Rome in her worst days could scarcely equal." MYERS, A. H., pp. 276, 292.

5—U
"Upon the partition of the empire of Alexander, Ptolemy had received Egypt, with parts of Arabia and Libya. To these he added by conquest of Syria, Phoenicia, Palestine, Cyrene, and Cyprus. Following the usage of the time, he transported a hundred thousand Jews from Jerusalem to Alexandria, attached them to his person and policies by wise and conciliatory measures and thus effected, in such measure as was possible, at this great capital of the Nile, that fusion of the races of the East and West which was the dream of Alexander." MYERS, A. H. p. 291. JOSEPHUS, Ant. 12-1-1.

5—V
"Sennacherib now pressed on against Egypt. . . . The condition of Egypt at this time was peculiar. . . . The second great battle between the Assyrians and Egyptians took place near the place called Altaku, which is no doubt the Eltekeh of the Jews, a small town in the vicinity of Elkron. Again the might of Africa yielded to that of Asia. The Egyptians and Ethiopians were defeated with great slaughter. Many chariots, with their drivers, both Egyptian and Ethiopian, fell into the hands of the conqueror, who also

took alive several 'sons' of the principal Egyptian monarch. The princes and chiefs who had been concerned in the revolt he took alive and slew, exposing their bodies on stakes round the whole circuit of the city walls. Great numbers of inferior persons, who were regarded as guilty of rebellion, were sold as slaves." Rawlinson's ANCIENT MONARCHIES, Vol. 2, pp. 159 and 160.

5—W
"The government had a general control over the main cuttings, opening and closing them according to certain fixed rules, which had for their object the fair and equitable distribution of the water supply over the whole territory. Each farmer received in turn sufficient to fill his own main reservoir, and from this by a network of water-courses continually diminishing in size the fluid was conveyed wherever needed, and at last brought to the very roots of the plants. The removal or replacing of a little mud, with the hand or with the foot, turned the water hither and thither, at the pleasure of the husbandman, who distributed it as his crops required.' Rawlinson's HISTORY OF ANCIENT EGYPT, Vol. 1, p. 84.

5—X
"A sort of light canoe, formed (we are told) of the papyrus plant, and propelled either by a single paddle or by a punting-pole, furnished the ordinary means of transport from one side of the Nile to the other, and was also used by fishermen in their occupation, and by herdsmen, when it was necessary to save cattle from an excessive inundation. The stem and stern of these vessels rose considerably above the water; they must have been flat-bottomed and broad, like punts, or they could have possessed no stability. They are probably the 'vessels of bulrushes,' spoken of by Isaiah, which were common to the Egyptians with the Ethiopians." RAWLINSON—HISTORY OF ANCIENT EGYPT. Vol. 1, p. 236.

5—Y
"There was a certain woman that dwelt beyond Jordan, her name was Mary; her father was Elezzar, of the village Bethezub, which signified the house of Hyssop. She was eminent for her family and her wealth, and had fled away to Jerusalem with the rest of the multitude, and was with them besieged therein at this time. The other effects of this Woman had been already seized upon; such I mean as she had brought with her out of Pereah, and removed to the city. What she had treasured up besides, also what food she had contrived to save, had been also carried off by the rapacious guards, who came every day running into her house for that purpose. This put the poor woman into a very great passion, and by the frequent, reproaches and imprecations she east at these rapacious villains, she had provoked them to anger against her; but none of them, either out of indignation she had raised against herself, or out of the commiseration of her case, would take away her life; and if she found any food, she perceived her labors were for others and not for herself; and it was now become impossible for her any way to find any more food, while the famine pierced through her very bowels and marrow, when also her passion was fired to a degree beyond the famine itself; nor did she consult with anything but with her passion and the necessity she was in. She then attempted a most unnatural thing; and snatching up her son, who was a child sucking at her breast, and said, 'O, thou miserable infant; for whom shall I preserve thee in this war, this famine, and this sedition? As to the war with the Romans, if they preserve our lives, we must be slaves. This famine also will destroy us, even before that slavery comes upon us, yet are these seditious rogues more terrible than both the other. Come one; be thou my food, and be thou a fury to these seditions varlets and a by-word to the world, which is all that is now wanting to complete the calamities of us Jews.' As soon as she had said this she slew her son; and then roasted him, and ate the one half of him, and kept the other half by her concealed. Upon this the seditious came in presently, and smelling the horrid scent of this food, they threatened her, that they would cut her throat immedi-

ately if she did not show them what food she had gotten already. She replied, that she had saved a very fine portion of it for them; and withal uncovered what was left of her son. Hereupon they were seized with a horror and amazement of mind, and stood astonished at the sight; when she said to them, 'This is mine own son; and what hath been done was mine own doing. Come eat of this food; for I have eaten of it myself. Do not you pretend to be either more tender than a woman, or more compassionate than a mother; but if you be so scrupulous, and do abominate this my sacrifice, as I have eaten the one half, let the rest be reserved for me also.' After which, those men went out trembling, being never so much affrighted at anything as they were at this, and with some difficulty they left the rest of that meat to the mother. Upon which the whole city was full of this horrid action immediately; and while every body laid this miserable case before their own eyes, they trembled, as if this unheard-of action had been done by themselves. So those that were thus distressed by the famine were desirous to die; and those already dead were esteemed happy, because they had not lived long enough either to hear or to see such miseries." JOSEPHUS—Wars, 6-3-4.

5—Z
Malachi was the last writer of the Old Testament, and wrote about 400 years before Christ, as is shown by the date herewith cited as follows:

INTERNATIONAL CYCLOPEDIA, Vol. 9. Article—
   MALACHI.
MYERS, ANCIENT HISTORY, page 245.
ROLLIN'S, Ancient History, Vol. 2, page 159. Plan of 1st
   and 3rd chapters of Book 7.
Horne's Introduction, Vol. 1, page 31—Footnote also p. 21.
HISTORICAL REFERENCE BOOK—Heilprin, page 482.
Prideaux, Ano. 409.

6—A

"The passage of Demosthenes above alluded to occurs in his first oration against Philip of Macedon, and is noticed by Longinus (sect. 18) as a fine specimen of the use of interrogations in the sublime—'Is it' says the orator, 'Is it your sole ambition to wander through the public places, each inquiring of the other, what news? Can any thing be more new than that a man of Macedon should conquer the Athenians and give law to Greece?' (Oratores Gracei, a Reiske, tom, 1. p. 43) Towards the close of Demosthenes' oration on Philip's letter to the Athenians, the orator speaking of the successes of Philip, has the following passage: 'How is it that, in the late war, his arms had such superior fortune? This is the cause (for I will speak with undaunted freedom), he takes the field himself; endures its toils and shares its dangers; no favorable incident escapes him. While we (for the truth must not be concealed) are confined within our walls with perfect in activity, delaying, and voting, and inquiring in the public places, whether there is anything new. Can anything better deserve the name of new, than that a Macedonian should insult Athens'?"

Quoted by HORNE, Introduction, Vol. 1, p. 80—note.

6—B

"No altar with this inscription (TO THE UNKNOWN GOD) has come down to our times; but we know, from the express testimony of Lucian, that there was such an inscription at Athens. The occasion of this altar being erected, in common with many others bearing the same inscription, is thus related by Diogenes Laertius: The Athenians, being afflicted with a pestilence, invited Epimenides to lustrate their city. The method adopted by him was, to carry several sheep to the Areopagus; whence they were left to wander as they pleased, under the observation of persons to attend them. As each sheep lay down, it was sacrificed on the spot to the propitious God. By this ceremony, it is said, the deity was relieved; but, as it was still unknown what deity was propitious, an altar was erected to the unknown God on every spot where a sheep had been sacrificed. HORNE, Introduction, Vol. 1, p. 90.

6—C
"The copies of the law must be transcribed from ancient manuscripts of approved character only with pure ink, on parchment prepared from the hide of a clean animal, for this express purpose by a Jew, and fastened together by the strings of clean animals; every skin, must contain a certain number of columns of prescribed length and breadth, each column comprising a given number of lines and words; no word must be written by heart or with points, or without being first pronounced orally by the copyist; the name of God is not to be written but with the utmost devotion and attention, and previously to writing it, he must wash his pen. The want of a single letter, or the redundance of a single letter, the writing of prose as verse, or verse as prose, respectively vitiates a manuscript; and when a copy has been completed, it must be examined and corrected within thirty days after the writing has been finished, in order to determine whether it is to be approved or rejected. These rules, it is said, are observed to the present day by the persons who transcribe the sacred writings for the use of the Synagogue." HORNE, Introduction, Vol. 1, p. 217.

6—D
"During the seventy years captivity, though it does not appear that the Hebrews entirely lost their native tongue, yet it underwent so considerable change from their adoption of the vernacular languages of the countries where they had resided, that afterwards, on their return from exile, they spoke a dialect of Chaldee mixed with Hebrew words. On this account it was that, when the Hebrew scriptures were read, it was found necessary to interpret them to the people in the Chaldean language; as, when Ezra the scribe brought the book of the law of Moses before the congregation, the Levites are said to have caused the people to understand the law, because they read in the book, in the law of God distinct-

ly, and gave the sense, and caused them to understand the reading." HORNE, Introduction, Vol. 1, p. 190.

6—E
"A twofold order of arrangement of the sacred books is observable in the Hebrew manuscripts, viz, the Talmudical and the Masoretic. Originally, the different books of the Old Testament were not joined together; according to Rabbi Elias Levite (the most learned Jewish writer on the subject), they were first joined together by the members of the great synagogue, who divided them into three parts—the law, the prophets, and Hagiographa." HORNE, Introduction, Vol. 1, p. 217.

6—F
"The violence of persecution was another most formidable obstacle to the propagation of the Christian religion. In fact, from its first origin to the time of Constantine, Christianity, with the exception of a few short intervals, was subjected to the most violent persecutions. At Jerusalem the apostles were imprisoned, scourged, or put to death in various ways. Wherever they directed their steps, they were pursued by the Jews, who either accused them before the Jewish and Heathen tribunal or stirred up the populace against them. But these persecutions were comparatively, only slight fore-runners of those which succeeding ages witnessed; and ecclesiastical history (which is corroborated by heathen writers as well as by heathen edicts and inscriptions that are still extant) records ten grievous general persecutions of the Christians under the pagan emperors, within the space of two hundred and fifty years." HORNE, Introduction, Vol. 1, p. 449.

6—G
"The propriety of this (statement of Jeremiah, 49:19) will appear, when it is known that in ancient times the river Jordan was particularly infested with lions, which concealed themselves among the thick reeds upon its banks, let us then imagine one of these monarchs of the dessert asleep among the thickets upon the

banks of that river; let us further suppose him to be suddenly awakened by the roaring, or dislodged by the overflowing of the rapid, tumultuous torrent, and in his fury rushing into the upland country; and we shall perceive the admirable propriety and force of the prophet's allusion." "After having descended," says Maundrell, "the outermost bank of Jordan, yon go about a furlong upon a level strand before yon come to the immediate bank of the river. This second bank is so beset with bushes and trees, such as tamarisks, willows, oleanders, etc, that you can see no water, till you have made your way through them. In this thicket anciently, and the same is reported of it at this day, several sorts of wild beasts were wont to harbor themselves; whose being washed out of the covert by the overflowing of the river gave occasion to that allusion, He shall come up like a lion from the swelling of Jordan." HORNE, Introduction, Vol. 1, p. 368, and note.

6—H
"The ancients generally, and the Jews in particular, accounting the bowels to be the seat of sympathy and the tender passions, applied the organ to the sense—Kuinoel in loc, has given illustrations from classical writers, and also from the Apocrypha." HORNE, Introduction, Vol. 1, p. 328.

6—I
"According to these notices, (of Asshur-bani-pal concerning his father, Esar-haddon) it would appear that Esar-haddon, having entered Egypt with a large army, probably in B. C. 670, gained a great battle over the forces of Tirhakah in the lower country, and took Memphis, the city where the Ethiopian held his court, after which he proceeded southwards, and conquered the whole of the Nile valley as far as the southern boundary of the Theban district. Thebes itself was taken; and Tirhakah retreated into Ethiopia. Esar-haddon thus became master of all Egypt, at least as far as Thebes, or Diospolis, the No or No-Amon of Scripture." RAWLINSON'S ANCIENT MONARCHES. Vol. 2, p. 193.

6—J

ARAMAIC LANGUAGES are so called from ARAM, a geographical term which in old Semetic usage designates nearly the same districts as the Greek word, Syria. Aram, however, does not include Palestine while it comprehends Mesopotamia (Heb. Aram of two rivers), a region which the Greeks frequently distinguish from Syria proper. Thus, the Aramaic languages may be geographically defined as the Semitic dialects originally current in Mesopotamia and the regions extending S. W. from the Euphrates to Palestine." BRITANICA, Vol. 2, p. 307.

"Etymologically, 'Syria' is merely an abbreviation of 'Assyria,' a name which covered the subject lands of the Assyrian empire, the subject-people being also called 'Syrians.' Afterwards, in the Graeco-Roman period, the shorter word came to be restricted to the territory west of the Euphrates, the designation 'Syrians,' however, being given to the great mass of the Semitic populations dwelling between the Tigris and the Mediterranean, who are more accurately called Aramaeans." BRITANNICA, 22-821, "Aram, which occurs in Scripture with the same frequency as Asshur, is like Asshur, a name concerning the application of which there is no doubt. Our translators almost always render the word, as did the Septuagint interpreters, by 'Syria' and the term though etymologically quite distinct, is beyond a doubt, in its use by the Hebrews, a near equivalent for the 'Syria' of the Greeks and Romans. It designates a people distinct from, yet closely allied with, the Assyrians, which, in the remotest times whereto history reaches, was established in the valley of the middle Euphrates, and in the tract between the Euphrates and the Mediterranean. This people, known to itself as Aramaean, continued the predominant race in the country to the time of the Mohammedan conquest." RAWLINSON, Origin of National, p. 234.

"Between the outer limits of the Syro-Arabian desert and the foot of the great mountain range of Kurdistan and Luristan intervenes a territory long famous in the world's history, and the chief site of three out of five empires of whose history, geography, and antiquities it is proposed to treat in the present volumes. Known to the Jews as Aram-Naharaim, or 'Syria of the two rivers'; to the Greeks and Romans as Mesopotamia, or 'the between-river country." Rawlinson, Five Great Monarchies, Vol. 1, p. 2. See also, in same volume, pp. 43, 179, 236, 262.

6—K
"Parturition in the East is unusually easy. The office of a midwife is thus, in many Eastern countries, in little use, but is performed, when necessary, by relatives. In the description of the transaction in Ex. 1: one expression, 'upon the stools' receives remarkable illustration from modern usage. The Egyptian practice, as described by Mr. Lane, exactly answers to that indicated in the book of Exodus. 'Two or three days before the expected time of delivery, the Layeh,' (midwife) 'conveys to the house the kursee el-wiladeh, a chair of a peculiar form upon which the patient is to be seated during the birth.'" SMITH'S BIBLE DICTIONARY, Article—MIDWIFE.

6—L
"All the flat thereon Babylon stood being by reason of so many rivers and canals running through it, made in many places marshy, especially near the said rivers and canals, this caused it to abound much in willows; and, therefore, it is called, in scripture, the valley of willows, (for so the words, Isa. 15:7, which we translate the book of the willows, ought to be rendered; and, for the same reason, the Jews (Psa. 137:1, 2) are said, when they were by the rivers of Babylon, in the land of their captivity, to have hung 'their harps upon the willows, that is, because of the abundance of them which grew by these rivers." PRIDEAUX'S CONNEXION, Part 1, Bk. 1, An. 570.

6—M
"After the death of Belshazzar, Darius the Mede is said in scripture to have taken the kingdom: for Cyrus, as long as his uncle

lived, allowed him a joint title with him in the empire, although it was all gained by his own valor, and out of deference to him ye yielded him the first place honor in it. But the whole power of the army, and the chief conduct of all affairs being still in his hands, he only was looked on as the supreme governor of the empire, which he had erected; and therefore there is no notice at all taken of Darius in the Canon of Ptolemy, but immediately after the death of Belshazzar (who is there called Nabonadius) Cyrus is placed as the next successor, as in truth and reality he was; the other having no more than the name and the shadow' of the sovereignty, excepting only in Media, which was his own proper dominion." PRIDEAUX'S CONNEXION, Bk, 1, Pt. 2. An. 538.

6—N
"The difference that is between the true year of our Saviour's incarnation, and that of the vulgar era of it, proceeds from hence: that it was not till the five hundred and twenty-seventh year of that era that it was first brought into use. Dionysius Exiguus, a Scythian by birth, and then a Roman abbot, was the first author of it; and Beda our countryman, taking it from him, used it in all his writings; and the recommendation which he gave it thereby, hath made it in common use among Christians ever since, especially in these western parts. Had all Christians calculated their true time by it from the beginning of the church of Christ (as it could be wished they had) there could then have been no mistakes in it. But it being five hundred and twenty-seven years after Christ's incarnation before this era of it was ever used, no wonder, that, after so great a distance of time, a mistake was made in the filing of the first year of it." PRIDEAUX'S CONNEXION, Preface. Also see 10—A.

6—O
"When they (the Jews) saw the new moon, then they began their months, which sometimes consisted of twenty-nine days, and sometimes of thirty, according as the new moon did sooner or later appear. The reason of this was, because the Synodical course

of the moon (that is, from new moon to new moon) being twenty-nine days and a half day, which a month of twenty-nine days fell short of, was made up by adding it to the next month, which made it consist of thirty days; so that their months consisted of twenty-nine and thirty days alternately. None of them had fewer than twenty-nine days, and therefore they never looked for the new moon before the night following the twenty-ninth day; and, if they then saw it, the next day was the first day of the following month. Neither had any of their months more than thirty days, and therefore they never looked for the new moon after the night following the thirtieth day; but then, if they saw it not, they concluded, that the appearance was obstructed by the clouds, and made the next day the first of the following month, without expecting any longer; and of twelve of these months their common year consisted." PRIDEAUX'S CONNEXION, Preface.

6—P
"Although Ammon reigned but two years, yet the beginning of the reign of Josiah is here put at the distance of three years from the beginning of the first year of Ammon, because the odd months of the reign of Hezekiah, Manasseh, and Ammon, over and above the round number of years, which they are said to have reigned, do by this time amount to a whole year more, which the chronology of the ensuing history makes necessary to be here supposed." PRIDEAUX'S CONNEXION. An. 640.

6—Q
"But they (the nations sent in replace the tribes of Israel only took him (The God of Israel) hereon into the number of their former deities and worshiped him jointly with the gods of the nation from whence they came; and in this corruption of joining the worship of their false gods with that of the true they continued, till the building of the Samaritan temple on Mount Gerizim by Sanballat; but, on that occasion, abundance of Jews falling off to them, they reduced them from this idolatry to the worship of the true God only, as shall be hereafter related; and they have contin-

ued in the same worship ever since even to this day." PRIDEAUX'S CONNEXION, An. 676.

6—R
"Thus far Isaiah; and besides this, there are several other prophecies in the other prophets to the same purpose, which have been already taken notice of. It must be acknowledged that there is mention made of Babylon as of a city standing long after the time where I have placed its desolation, as in Lucan, Philostratus, and others. But in all those authors, and wherever else we find Babylon spoken of as a city in being after the time of Seleucus Nicator, it must be understood, not of old Babylon on the Euphrates, but of Seleucia on the Tigris. For as that succeeded in the dignity and grandeur of old Babylon, so also did it in its name. At first it was called Seleucia Babylonia that is, the Babylonic Seleucia, or Seleucia, of the province of Babylon, to distinguish it from the other Seleucias which were elsewhere, and after that Babylonia simply, and at length Babylon." PRIDEAUX'S CONNEXION, An. 293.

6—S
"For what the Jews call the great synagogue were a number of the elders amounting to one hundred and twenty, who succeeding after some others, in a continued series, from the return of the Jews again into Judea, after the Babylonish captivity, to the time of Simon the Just, labored in the restoring of the Jewish church and state in that country; in order whereto, the holy scriptures being the rule they were to go by, their chief care and study was to make a true collection of those scriptures, and publish them accurately to the people. Ezra, and the men of the great synagogue that lived in his time, completed the work as I have said. And as to what remained farther to be done in it, where can we better place the performing of it, and the ending and finishing of the whole thereby, than in that time where those men of the great synagogue ended that were employed therein, that is, in the time of Simon the Just, who was the last of them? And that, especially

since there are some particulars in those books which seem necessarily to refer down to the time as late as those of Alexander the Great, if not later. For, in the third chapter of the first book of Chronicles, we have the genealogy of the sons of Zerubbabel, carried down for so many descents after him, as may well be thought to reach the time of Alexander; and in the book of Nehemiah, chapter 12, verse 22, we have the days of Jaddua spoken of, as of days past; but Judah outlived Alexander two years. I acknowledge these passages, both put in after the time of Ezra, and after the time of- Nehemiah (who were the writers of those books), by those who completed the Canon. To say they were inserted by those holy men themselves who wrote the books, the chronology of their history will not bear; for then they must have lived down beyond those times which those passages refer us to; but this is inconsistent with what is written of them. And to say that they were put in by any other than those, who, by the direction of the Holy Spirit of God, completed the Canon of the scriptures, will be to derogate from their excellency; and, therefore we must conclude, that, since Simon the Just was the last of those-that were employed in this work, it was by him that the last finishing hand was put thereto, and that it was in his time, and under his presidency, and chiefly by his direction, that the Canon of the Holy Scriptures Of the Old Testament, by which we now receive them, was perfected, and finally settled in the Jewish church. And thus far having brought down this history through the scripture times, till the Canon of the Scriptures of the Old Testament, was fully perfected, I shall here end the first part of it. After this followed the Mishnical times, that is, the times of traditions. Hitherto the scriptures were the only rule of faith and manners which God's people studied; but thenceforth traditions began to be regarded, till at length they overbore the word of God itself, as we find in our Saviour's time. The collection of those traditions they call the Mishnah, that is, the second law, and those who delivered and taught them were styled the Mishnical doctors. From the time of Simon the Just their time began, and they continued to be known by that name, till Rabbi Judah Hakkadosh collected all those traditions together, and wrote them into the book which they call the Mishnah, which was done about one hundred and fifty years after Christ, as hath been above related. The ages in which they flourished, till the time of Christ, shall be the subject of the second part of this history." PRIDEAUX'S CONNEXION, An. 292. BRITTANNICA. Article—CANON.

6—T
"But here it is to be noted, that there were two sorts of proselytes among the Jews: 1. The proselytes of the gate; and, 2, the proselytes of justice. The former they obliged only to renounce idolatry, and worship God according to the law of nature, which they reduced to seven articles, called by them the seven precepts of the sons of Noah. To these, they held all men were obliged to conform, but not so as to the law of Moses; for this they reckoned as a law made only for their nation, and not for the whole world. As to the rest of mankind, if they kept the law of nature, and observed the precepts above mentioned, they held, that they performed all that God required of them, and would by this service render themselves as acceptable to him as the Jews by theirs. And therefore, they allowed all such to live with them in their land, and from hence they were called gerim toshavim, i. e. 'sojourning proselytes;' and for the same reason they were called also gere shahar, i. e. 'proselytes of the gate,' as being permitted to dwell with those of Israel within the same gates. The occasion of this name seemed to be taken from those words in the fourth commandment vegereka bishareka, i. e. 'and the strangers which are within thy gates,' which may as well be rendered, 'the proselytes which are within thy gates,' that is, the proselytes of the gate that dwell with thee; for the Hebrew word ger, a stranger, signifies also a proselyte; and both, in this place in the fourth commandment, come to the same thing; for no strangers were permitted to dwell within their gates, unless they renounced idolatry, and were proselyted so far as to the observance of the seven precepts of the sons of Noah. Though they were slaves taken in war, they were not permitted to live with them within any of the gates of Israel on

any other terms; but on their refusal thus far to comply, were either given up to the sword, or else sold to some foreign people. And, as who were thus far made proselytes were admitted to dwell with them, so also were they admitted into the temple, there to worship God; but were not allowed to enter any farther than into the outer court, called the court of the Gentiles, for, into the inner courts, which were within the enclosure called the Chel, none were admitted, but only such as were thorough professors of the whole Jewish religion: and therefore, when any of these sojourning proselytes came into the temple, they always worshipped in the outer court. And of this sort of proselytes Naaman the Syrian, and Cornelius the centurion, are held to have been. The other sort of proselytes, called the proselytes of justice, were such as took on them the observance of the whole Jewish law; for, although the Jews did not hold this necessary for such as were not of their nation, yet they refused none, but gladly received all who would thus profess their religion; and they are remarked in our Saviour's time to have been very sedulous to convert all they could hereto: and, when they were thus proselyted to the Jewish religion, they were initiated to it by baptism, sacrifice, and circumcision, and thenceforth were admitted to all the rites, ceremonies, and privileges that were used by the natural Jews." PRIDEAUX'S CONNEXION, An. 129.

6—U

"For the heresy of the Ebionites approached nearer the religion of the Jews than that of the orthodox Christians. They professed, indeed, to believe in Christ as the true Messiah, but held him to be no more than a mere man, and thought themselves still under the obligation of the law of Moses, and therefore were circumcised, and observed all the other rites and ceremonies of the Jewish religion; and, for this reason, they had commonly the name of Jews given them by the orthodox Christians."—PRIDEAUX'S CONNEXISON, An. 277.

6—V

"This punishment among the Jews was not to exceed forty stripes (Deut. 25:3) and therefore the whip with which it was inflicted being made with three thongs, and each blow giving three stripes, they never inflicted upon any criminal more than thirteen blows, because thirteen of those blows made thirty-nine stripes; and to add another blow, would be to transgress that law, by adding two stripes over and above forty, contrary to its prohibition. And in this manner was it that Paul, when whipped of the Jews, received forty stripes save one (2 Cor. 11:24) that is, thirteen blows with this threefold whip, which made thirty-nine stripes, i. e. forty save one." PRIDEAUX'S CONNEXION, An. 108. Note.

6—W

"The Sadducees say, that there is no resurrection, neither angel nor spirit, the Pharisees confess both, that is, first, that there is to be a resurrection from the dead; and, secondly, that there are angels and spirits. But according to Josephus, this resurrection of theirs was no more than a Pythagorean resurrection, that is, a resurrection of the soul only by its transmigration into another body, and born anew with it. But from this resurrection they excluded all that were notoriously wicked. For of such their notion was, that their souls, as soon as separated from their bodies, were transmitted into a state of everlasting woe, there to suffer the punishment of their sins to all eternity. But, as to lesser crimes, their opinion was, that they were punished in the bodies which the souls of those that committed them were next sent into. And according to this notion was it, that Christ's disciples asked him, in the ease of the man that was born blind, 'Who did sin, this man or his parents, that he was born blind?' For this plainly supposeth an antecedent state of being, otherwise it cannot be conceived, that a man could sin before he was born. And, when the disciples told Christ that some said of him, that he was Elias, and others Jeremias, or some of the prophets; this can be understood no otherwise, but that they thought according to the doctrine of the transmigration of souls, that he was come into the world with the would of Elias, or of Jeremias, or of some other of the old prophets transmitted into him, and born with him." PRIDEAUX'S CONNEXION, An. 107.

6—X
"This year was born Herod the Great, who was afterward king of Judea (for he was twenty-five years old when he was first made governor of Galilee in the year before Christ 47). His father was Antipas, a noble Idumaean, and his mother Cyprus of an illustrious family among the Arabians. . . . By country therefore he was an Idumaean, but by religion a Jew, as all other Idumaeans were from the time that Hycranus brought them all to embrace the Jewish religion, of which I have above given an account." PRIDEAUX'S CONNEXION, An. 72.

"The civil government of Judea at the time of Christ's birth, was vested in the hands of A Roman stipendiary, named Herod the Great—a title to which he could have no pretentions, except from the magnitude of his vices. Nature, it is true, had not with held from him the talent requisite for a lofty and brilliant course of life; but such was his jealous disposition, such the ferocity of his temper, his devotedness to luxury, pomp, and magnificence so madly extravagant, and so much beyond his means, in short, so extensive and enormous was the catalogue of his vices, that he became an object of utter detestation to the afflicted people over whom he swayed the kingly sceptre. Instead of cherishing and protecting his subjects, he appears to have made them sensible of his authority merely by oppression and violence; so that they complained to the Emperor Augustus, at Rome of his cruelties, declaring that they had suffered as much as if a wild beast had reigned over them; and Eusebius affirms that the cruelty of this nefarious despot far surpassed whatever had been represented in tragedy. Herod was not ignorant of the hatred which he had drawn upon himself, but to soften its asperity he became a professed devotee to the Jewish religion, and at a vast expense restored their temple which through age had fallen into decay; but the effect of all this was destroyed by his still conforming to the manners and habits of those who worshipped a plurality of gods; and so many things were countenanced in direct opposition to the Jewish religion, that the hypocrisy of the tyrant's professions were too manifest to admit of a doubt.—JONES' CHURCH HISTORY, Introduction, Part II.

6—Y
"From the Church fund, which was formed by the voluntary contributions of every member of the Church, at every Sunday service, or, as in the North African Church, on the first Sunday of every month, a part was used for the pay of the spiritual order." NEANDER'S CHURCH HISTORY, Section 2.

6—Z
"The usual sort of bread which was brought by the members of the Church, was used for the Supper of the Lord. Justin Martyr calls it expressly, 'common bread,' (koinos artos). Those who went on the supposition that Christ celebrated the festival of the Passover a day earlier than usual, had no reason at all to use anything but the common sort of bread in the celebrating of the Lord's Supper; and even those who were of a different opinion, did not think the use of unleavened bread an essential part of the performance of this rite. We find, however, one exception in the case of some Judaizing Christians, which arose from the very nature of the ease; for as they kept a festival in commemoration of that Last Supper of our Lord, only once a year at the Passover, it naturally happened that, as Christians who were continuing in the observance of the Jewish ceremonial law, they would eat unleavened bread. As among the ancients, and especially in the East, it was not customary to drink pure wine, unmixed with water, at meal tunes, it was hence supposed that Christ also used wine mixed with water." NEANDER'S CHURCH HISTORY, Section III.

7—A
"There was, however, as Origen justly represented in reply to Celsus, a great difference in the manner which those persons (enchanters) used, from that made use of by the preachers of the Gospel. Those deceivers flattered the sinful inclinations of men, and forming themselves upon their then habits of thinking they required no sacrifices from their followers of anything dear to them. On the contrary, he who, in the earlier ages, would become a Christian, must tear himself away from many of his darling passions, and be ready to sacrifice every thing for his faith." NEANDER'S CHURCH HISTORY, Section I.

7—B
"By means of letters and of brethren who traveled about, even the most remote Churches of the Roman empire were connected together. When a Christian arrived in a strange town, he first inquired for the Church, (Gemeinde, literally congregation,) and he was here received as a brother, and provided with everything needful for his spiritual or corporeal substance. But since deceivers, spies with evil intentions, and false teachers, who sought only to propagate their unevangelical doctrines among the simple-minded Christians, abused the confidence and the kindness of Christians, some measures of precaution became necessary, in order to avert the many injuries which might result from this conduct. An arrangement was, therefore, introduced, that only such traveling Christians should be received, as brethren, into Churches where they were strangers, as could produce a testimonial from the bishop of the Church from which they came. They called these Church letters." NEANDER'S CHURCH HISTORY, Section II.

7—C
"Notwithstanding the dissatisfaction at first manifested by the people of Rome, Adrian VI, repaired to that city in the month of August, 1522, and was well received. It was reported that he had more than five thousand benefices in his gift, and every man

reckoned on having his share. For many years the papal throne had not been filled by such a pontiff. Just, active, learned, pious, sincere, and of irreproachable morals, he permitted himself to be blinded neither by favor nor passion. He followed the middle course traced out by Erasmus, and in a book reprinted at Rome during his pontificate, he said, 'It is certain that the pope may err in matters of faith, in defending heresy by his opinions or decretals.' This is indeed a remarkable assertion for a pope to make; and if the ultra-montanists reply that Adrian was mistaken on this point, by this very circumstance they affirm what they deny, viz. the fallibility of the popes." D'AUBIGNE'S HISTORY OF THE REFORMATION. Bk. 10, chapter 2.

7—D
"What they attack in a general sense is the confusion of the two societies (Church and State); what they demand, is their independence, I do not say their separation, for separation of Church and State was quite unknown to the reformers." D'AUBIGNE'S HISTORY OF THE REFORMATION, Book 14, Chapter 7.

7—E
"The Church, though consisting wholly of Hebrews, comprised two classes of persons; one party understood only the Hebrew and Chaldee languages, which was used in their synagogues at Jerusalem and its vicinity, while the other had been accustomed chiefly to the use of the Greek language, into which the Old Testament scriptures had been translated, (the version which we now call the Septuagint), and which had been for some time in common use, previous to the coming of Christ, in all the Jewish synagogues dispersed throughout the cities of Greece, as well as Egypt, These last were called Hellenists or Grecians." JONES' CHURCH HISTORY, Chapter 1, Section 2.

7—F
"At this time, (in the reign of Domitian) the apostle John was banished to the island of Patmos, from whence he wrote his epis-

tles to the seven churches in Asia. He is said to have survived the persecution of Domitian, though it is uncertain how long; and to have died at Ephesus in the reign of Nerva or Trajan, at which city he was buried." JONES' CHURCH HISTORY, Chapter 1. Section 6.

7—G
"Finding all other resources ineffectual, the emperor was at length under the necessity of issuing letters to the bishops of the several provinces of the empire, enjoining them to assemble together at Nice, in Bithynia, which was accordingly done, A. D. 325. This is what goes by the name of 'the first general council.' The number of bishops was three hundred and eighteen, besides a multitude of presbyters, deacons, Aneolithic's, and others, amounting in the whole to two thousand and forty-eight persons.

"To everything that was said, he (the emperor) gave a patient hearing, and by his mildness and great address, speaking to them in Greek (which he was in some measure able to do) he at length prevailed upon them to come to an agreement, says Eusebius, not only with respect to their private differences, but also with regard to the two great objects of their assembling—the rule of faith as it respected the Arian controversy, and the time of celebrating Easter." Council began June 19, closed Aug. 25th. JONES' HISTORY, Chapter 3, See. 1.

7—H
"When the undivided government of the empire centered in the hands of Constantius he evinced a strong predilection for the Arian side of the controversy, and Arianism became fashionable at court. The emperor favored only the bishops of that party. Paul, the orthodox prelate of the see of Constantinople, was ejected from his office by the emperor's order, and Macedonius substituted in his room. This man adopted a scheme different from either party, and contended that the Son was not consubstantial, but of a like substance, with the Father, openly propagating this new

theory, after thrusting himself into the bishoprick of Paul; and thus, by the addition of a single letter, affecting to settle the whole dispute. Frivolous as was this distinction, it enraged the orthodox party, who, filled with rage and resentment, rose in a body to oppose Hermogenes, the officer whom Constantine had sent to introduce unto his episcopal throne, burnt down his house, and drew him round the streets by his heels until they had murdered him." JONES' CHURCH HISTORY, Chapter 3, Section 2.

7—I
"This trying state of things was continued with more or less intermission, during the reigns of Gallus, Valerian, Diocletian, and others of the Roman emperors; but the detail is harassing to the feelings, and instead of prosecuting it circumstantially, I shall dismiss the subject by an extract from Dr. Chandler's History of Persecutions, relating to this period. 'The most excessive and outrageous barbarities,' says he, 'were made use of upon all who would not blaspheme Christ and offer incense to the imperial gods. They were publicly whipped—drawn' by the heels through the streets of cities—racked till every bone of their body was disjointed—had their teeth beat out—their noses, hands, and ears cut off—sharp pointed spears run under their nails—were tortured with melted lead thrown on their naked bodies—had their eyes dug out—their limbs cut off—were condemned to the mines—ground between stones—stoned to death—burnt alive—thrown headlong from the high buildings—beheaded, smothered in burning lime kilns—run through the body with sharp spears—destroyed with hunger, thirst, and cold—thrown to the wild beasts—broiled on gridirons with slow fires—cast by heaps into the sea—crucified—scraped to death with sharp shells—torn in pieces by the boughs of trees—and, in a word, destroyed by all the various methods that the most diabolical subtlety and malice could advise.'" JONES' CHURCH HISTORY, Chapter 2, Section 3. Quoted from Dr. Chandler's History of Persecutions.

7—J

"The scriptures were now (fourth century) no longer the standard of the Christian faith. What was orthodox and what heterodox, was, from henceforward, to be determined by the decisions of fathers and councils; and religion propagated not by the apostolic methods of persuasion, accompanied with the meekness and gentleness of Christ, but by imperial edicts and decrees; nor were gainsayers to be brought to convictions by the simple weapons of reason and scripture, but persecuted and destroyed."—JONES' CHURCH HISTORY, Chap. 3, Sec. 2.

7—K

"It may be proper to remark that long before (the times of which we now treat (fourth century) some Christians had seen it their duty to withdraw from the communion of the church of Rome. The first instance of this that we find on record, if we except that of Tertullian, is the ease of Novatian, who in the year 251, was ordained the pastor of a church in the city of Rome, which maintained no fellowship with the catholic party. On the death of bishop Fabian, Cornelius, a brother elder, and a violent partisan for taking in the multitude, was put in nomination. Novatian opposed him; but as Cornelius carried his election and he saw no prospect of reformation, but on the contrary a tide of immorality pouring into the church he withdrew and a great many with him. . . . In the end Novatian formed a church, and was elected bishop. Great numbers followed his example, and all over the empire Puritan churches were constituted and flourished through the succeeding two hundred years. Afterwards, when penal laws obliged them to lurk in corners, and worship God in private, they were distinguished by a variety of names, and a succession of them continued till the Reformation.

"They call Novatian the author of heresy of puritanism; and yet they know that Tertullian had quitted the church near fifty years before, for the same reason, and Privates, who was an old man in the time of Novatian had, with several more repeatedly remonstrated against the alterations taking place; and, as they could get no redress had dissented and formed separate congregations." JONES' CHURCH HISTORY, Chapter 3, Section 2, being a quotation from Robinson by Jones.

"It is happy for simple Christians that their rule of duty is plain, though, unfortunately, not sanctioned by either catholic or the reformed church. It is 'not to admit into the worship of God, anything which is neither not expressly commanded, or plainly exemplified in the New Testament.' This was evidently the principle upon which Arius proceeded in opposing the superstitions of his time, (5th century) and for which he deserves to be held.in perpetual remembrance." (Same author, Chapter 3, Sec. 3.)

7—L
"About the year 318, while Alexander was bishop of Alexandria, the Arian controversy broke out in the city and the whole Eastern Church was soon involved in the strife. We cannot enter here into a discussion of Arius' views; but in order to understand the rapidity with which the Arian party grew, and the strong hold which it possessed from the very start in Syria and Asia Minor, we must remember that Arius was not himself the author of that system which we know as Arianism, but that he learned the essentials of it from his instructor Lucian. The latter was one of the most learned men of his age in the Oriental Church, and founded an exegetical-theological school in Antioch which for a number of years stood outside of the communion of the orthodox Church in that city, but shortly before the martyrdom of Lucian himself (which took place in 311 or 312) made its peace with tin Church, and was recognized by it. He was held in the highest reverence by his . . . . and exerted a. great influence over them even after his death. Among them were such men as Arius, Eusebius of Nicomedia, Asterius, and others who were afterward known as staunch Arianists. According to Harnack the chief points in the system of Lucian and his disciples were the creation of the Son, the denial of his co-eternity with the Father, and his immutability

acquired by persistent progress and steadfastness. His doctrine, which differed from that of Paul of Sarno chiefly in the fact that it was not a man but a created heavenly being who became 'Lord,' was evidently the result of a combination of the teaching of Paul and of Origen. It will be seen that we have here, at least in germ, all the essential elements of Arianism proper: the creation of the Son out of nothing, and consequently the conclusion that there was a time when he was not; the distinction of his essence from that of the Father, but at the same time the emphasis upon the fact that he 'was created as the other creatures,' and is therefore to be sharply distinguished from them." PROLEGOMENA to Eusebius, p. 11, Article 5.

"Rushing in the opposite extreme (From Sabellianism) he (Arius) maintained, that the Son was totally and essentially distinct from the Father; that he was the first and noblest of those beings, whom God had created out of nothing, the instrument by whose subordinate operation the Almighty Father formed the universe, and therefore inferior to the Father, both in nature and in dignity." MOSHEIM, Cen 4, Pt. 2, C. 5, See. 10.

"The occasion of this dispute, which is well-known by the name of 'The Arian Controversy,' seems to have been simply this: Alexander, one of the prelates of that church, speaking upon the subject of the Trinity, had affirmed that there was 'an unity in the Trinity, and, particularly that the Son was coeternal, and consubstantial, and of the same dignity with the Father.' Arius objected to this language, and argued that 'If the Father begat the Son, he who was begotten must have a being of his existence; and from hence,' says he, 'he manifest that there was a time when he (the son) was not.'" JONES' CHURCH HISTORY, Chapter 3, Section 1.

"ARIUS, one of the most famous heretics; born about 256, in Libya (according to others, in Alexandria), died 336, at Constantinople. He was educated by Lucian, presbyter in the Church of

Alexandria when the Arian controversy with Bishop Alexander began (about 318) concerning the eternal deity of Christ and his equality with the Father (homoiousia) which he denied, holding that Christ was of a different essence, and a creature of the Father, though created before the world." Schaff-Herzog Encyclopedia, Article—ARIUS.

"The Church Council of Nicaea (A. D. 325)—With the view of harmonizing the different sects that had sprung up among the Christians and to settle the controversy between the Arians and the Athanasians respecting the nature of Christ,—the former denied his equality with God the Father,—Constantine called the first Ecumenical or General Council of the Church at Nicaea, a town in Asia Minor, A. D. 325. Arianism was denounced, and a formula of Christian faith adopted, which is known as the Nicene Creed." MYERS' ANCIENT HISTORY, Revised Ed. Page 526.

"The following are the terms of the (Nicene) Creed: 'We believe in one God, the Father Almighty, maker of all things, both visible and invisible; and in one Lord, Jesus Christ, the Son of God, begotten of the Father, only begotten, that is to say of the substance of the Father, God of God and Light of Light, very God of very God, begotten, not made, being of one substance with the Father (Homoousion to patri) by whom all things were made, both things in heaven and things on earth; who, for us men and for our salvation, came down and was made flesh, made man, suffered and rose again on the third day, went up into the heavens, and is to come again to judge the quick and the dead, and in the Holy Ghost.'

Then followed the clauses anathematizing the several assertions of the Arians, that 'there was a time when He (Jesus Christ) was not'—'before He was begotten He was not,'—'He came into existence from what was not,' and 'that He is of a different person' or 'substance' (Heteras hupostaseos e ousias).

This the original form of the Nicene Creed it will be observed, differs considerably from what is popularly known as the Nicene Creed. Afterwards certain clauses (which we have marked in italics) were omitted, and others of more importance added, especially the present conclusion of the creed, following the simple statement in the original of belief in the Holy Ghost.

"I believe in the Holy Ghost (the Lord and Giver of the life) who proceeded from the Father (and the Son), who with the Father and the Son are worshipped and glorified who spake by the prophets. And I believe the one Catholic and Apostolic Church. I acknowledge one baptism for the remission of sins. And I look for the resurrection of the, dead, and the life of the world to come." BRITANNICA, Vol. 6, Article—CREEDS.

7—M
"Festus was sent by Nero to be Felix's successor. Under him Paul, having made his defense, was sent bound to Rome. Aristarchus was with him, whom he also somewhere in his epistles quite naturally calls his fellow-prisoner. And Luke, who wrote the Acts of the Apostles, brought his history to a close at this point, after stating that Paul spent two whole years at Rome as a prisoner at large, and preached the word of God without restraint. Thus, after he had made his defense, it is said that the apostle was sent again upon the ministry of preaching, and that upon coming to the same city a second time he suffered martyrdom. In this imprisonment he wrote his second epistle to Timothy, in which he mentions his first defense and his impending death. But hear his testimony on these matters: 'At my first answer,' he says, 'no man stood with me, but all men forsook me: I pray God that it may not be laid to their charge. Notwithstanding the Lord stood with me, and strengthened me; that by me the preaching might be fully known, and that all the Gentiles might hear: and I was delivered out of the mouth of the lion.' He plainly indicates in these words that on the former occasion, in order that the preaching might be fulfilled by him, he was rescued from the mouth of the lion, refer-

ring, in this expression, to Nero, as is probable on account of the latter's cruelty. He did not therefore afterward add the similar statement: 'He will rescue me from the mouth of the lion'; for he saw in the spirit that his end would not be long delayed. Wherefore he adds the words, 'And he delivered me from the mouth of the lion,' this sentence: 'The Lord will deliver me from every evil work and will preserve me unto his heavenly kingdom,' indicating his speedy martyrdom which he also foretells still more clearly in the same epistle, when he writes, 'For I am now ready to be offered, and the time of my departure is at hand.' In his second epistle to Timothy, moreover, he indicates that Luke was with him when he wrote, but at his first defense not even he. Whence it is probable that Luke wrote the Acts of the Apostles at that time, continuing his history down to the period when he was with Paul. But these things have been adduced by us to show that Paul's martyrdom did not take place at the time of that Roman sojourn which Luke records. It is probable indeed that as Nero was more disposed to mildness in the beginning, Paul's defense of his doctrine was more easily received, but that when he had advanced to the commission of lawless deeds of daring, he made the apostles as well as others the subjects of his attacks." EUSEBIUS, Church History, Book 2, Chapter 22.

7—N
"The Roman Tertullian is likewise a witness of this. He writes as follows: 'Examine your records. There you will find that Nero was the first that persecuted this doctrine, particularly then when after subduing all the east, he exercised his cruelty against all at Rome. We glory in having such a man the leader in our punishment. For whoever knows him can understand that nothing was condemned by Nero unless it was something of great excellence.' Thus, publicly announcing himself as the first among God's chief enemies, he was led on to the slaughter of the apostles. It is, therefore, recorded that Paul was beheaded in Rome itself, and that Peter likewise was crucified under Nero. This account of Peter and Paul is substantiated by the fact that their names are pre-

served in the cemeteries of that place even to the present day." EUSEBIUS, Church History, Book 2, Chapter 25.

"Peter appears to have preached in Pontus, Galatia, Bithynia, Cappadocia, and Asia to the Jews of the dispersion. And at last, having come to Rome, he was crucified head-downwards; for he had requested that he might suffer in this way." EUSEBIUS, Church History, Book 3, Chapter 1.

7—O

"In addition to these he (Ignatius) wrote also to the church at Rome, entreating them not to secure his release from martyrdom, and thus rob him of his earnest hope. In confirmation of what has been said it is proper to quote briefly from this epistle. He writes as follows: 'From Syria even unto Rome I fight with wild, beasts, by land and by sea, by night and by day, being bound amidst ten leopards, that is, a company of soldiers who only become worse when they are well treated. In the midst of their wrongdoings, however, I am more fully learning discipleship, but I am not thereby justified. May I have joy of the beasts that are-prepared for me; and I pray that I may find them ready; I will even coax them to devour me quickly that they may not treat me as they have some whom they have refused to touch through fear. And if they are willing, I will compel them. Forgive me. I know what is expedient for me. Now do I begin to be a disciple. May naught of things visible and things invisible envy me; that I may attain unto Jesus Christ. Let fire and cross and attacks of wild beasts, let wrenching of bones, cutting of arms, crushing of the whole body, tortures of the devil let all these come upon me if only I may attain unto Jesus Christ.'" EUSEBIUS, Church History, Book 3, Chapter 36.

7—P

"But Polycarp, looking with dignified countenance upon the whole crowd that was gathered in the stadium waved his hand to them, and groaned, and raising his eyes toward heaven said,

'Away with the Atheists.' But when the magistrate pressed him, and said 'Swear, and I will release thee; revile Christ,' Polycarp said, 'Fourscore and six years have I been serving him, and he hath done me no wrong; how can I blaspheme my king who saved me?'" EUSEBIUS, Church History, Book 4, Chapter 15.

7—Q

"Accordingly the whole time of our Saviour's ministry is shown to have been not quite four full years, four high priests, from Annas to the accession of Caiaphas, having held office a year each. The Gospel therefore has rightly indicated Caiaphas as the high priest under whom the Saviour suffered." EUSEBIUS, Church History, Book 1, Chapter 10.

7—R

"If any one should assert all those who have enjoyed the testimony of righteousness, from Abraham himself back to the first man, were Christians in fact if not in name, he would not go beyond the truth. For that which the name indicates, that the Christian man, through the knowledge and the teaching of Christ, is distinguished for temperance and righteousness, for patience in life and manly virtue, and for a profession of piety toward the one and only God over all—all that was zealously practiced by them not less than by us. They did not care about circumcision of the body, neither do we. They did not care about observing Sabbaths, nor do we. They did not avoid certain kinds of food, neither did they regard the other distinctions which Moses first delivered to their posterity to be observed as symbols; nor do Christians of the present day do such things." EUSEBIUS, Church History, Book I. Chapter 4.

7—S

"For Matthew, who had at first preached to the Hebrews, when he was about to, go to other peoples, committed his Gospel to writing in his native tongue, and thus compensated those whom he was obliged to leave for the loss of his presence." "Since, in the beginning of this work, we promised to give, when needful, the words of the ancient presbyters and writers of the Church, in which they have declared those traditions which came down to them concerning the canonical books, and since Irenaeus was one of them, we will now give his words and, first, what he says of the sacred Gospel: 'Matthew published his Gospel among the Hebrews in their own language, etc.'" EUSEBIUS, Church History, Book 3, Chapter 25 and Book 5, Chapter 8.

7—T
"Accordingly he called on him with earnest prayer and supplications that he would reveal to him who he was, and stretch forth his right hand to help him in his present difficulties. And while he was thus praying with fervent entreaty a most marvelous sign appeared to him from heaven, the account of which it might have been hard to believe had it been related by any other persons. But since the victorious emperor himself long afterwards declared it to the writer of this history, when he was honored with his acquaintance and society, and confirmed his statement by an oath, who could hesitate to accredit the relation, especially since the testimony of after time has established its truth? He said that about noon, when the day was already beginning to decline, he saw with his own eyes the trophy of a cross of light in the heavens, above the sun, and bearing the inscription, CONQUER BY THIS. At this sight he himself was struck with amazement, and his whole army also, which followed him on this expedition, and witnessed the miracle." "He said, moreover, that he doubted within himself what the import of this apparition could be. And while he continued to ponder and reason on its meaning, night suddenly came on; then in his sleep the Christ of God appeared to him with the same sign which he had seen in the heavens, and commanded him to make a likeness of that sign which he had seen in the heavens, and to use it as a safeguard in all engagements with his enemies." "At dawn of day he arose, and communicated the marvel to his friends; and then calling together the workers in gold and precious stones, he sat in the midst of them,

and described to them the figure of the sign he had seen, bidding them represent it in gold and precious stones. And this representation I myself have had an opportunity of seeing,"—EUSEBIUS, Life of Constantine, Book 1, Chapters 28, 29, 30.

7—U
"Again, the sons of Greece celebrate Alexander the Macedonian as the conqueror of many and diverse nations; yet we find that he was removed by an early death, before he had reached maturity, being carried off by the effects of revelry and drunkenness. His whole life embraced but the space of thirty-two years, and his reign extended to no more than a third part of that period. Unsparing as the thunderbolt, he advanced through streams of blood and reduced entire nations and cities, young and old, to utter slavery. But when he had scarcely arrived at the maturity of life, and was lamenting the loss of youthful pleasures, death fell upon him with terrible stroke, and, that he might no longer outrage the human race, cut him off in a foreign and hostile land, childless, without successor, and homeless. His kingdom, too, was instantly dismembered, each of his officers taking away and appropriating a portion for himself. And yet this man is extolled for such deeds as these." EUSEBIUS, Life of Constantine, Book 1, Chap. 7.

7—V
"He ordained, too, that one day should be regarded as a special occasion for prayer; I mean that which is truly the first and chief of all, the day of our Lord and Saviour. The entire care of his household was entrusted to deacons and other ministers consecrated to the service of God, and distinguished by gravity of life and every other virtue; while his trusty body guard, strong in affection and fidelity to his person, found in their emperor an instructor in the practice of piety, and like him held the Lord's salutary day in honor, and performed on that day the devotions which he loved. The same observance was recommended by this blessed prince to all classes of his subjects; his earnest desire being gradually to lead all mankind to the worship of God. Accordingly, he

enjoined on all the subjects of the Roman empire to observe the Lord's day, as a day of rest, and also to honor the day which precedes the Sabbath; in memory, I suppose, of what the Saviour of mankind is recorded to have achieved on that day. And since his desire was to teach his whole army zealously to honor the Saviour's day (which derives its name from light, and from the sun), he freely granted to those among them who were partakers of the divine faith, leisure for attendance on the service of the Church of God, in order that they might be able, without impediment, to perform their religious worship." EUSEBIUS, Life of Constantine, Book 4, Chapter 18.

7—W
"Meantime, since there was no fear of capital punishment to deter from the commission of crime, for the emperor himself was uniformly inclined to clemency, and none of the provincial governors visited offenses with their proper penalties, this state of things drew with it no small degree of blame on the general administration of the empire; whether justly or not, let every one form his own judgment; for myself, I only ask permission to record the fact." EUSEBIUS, Life of Constantine, Book 4, Chapter 31.

7—X
"The evil demon, however, being unable to tear certain others from their allegiance to the Christ of God, yet found them susceptible in a different direction, and so brought them over to his own purposes. The ancients quite properly called these men EBIONITES, because they held poor and mean opinions concerning Christ. For they considered him a plain and common man, who was justified only because of his superior virtues, and who was the fruit of the intercourse of a man with Mary. In their opinion the observance of the ceremonial law was altogether necessary, on the ground that they could not be saved by faith in Christ alone and by a corresponding life. There were others, however, besides them, that were of the same name, but avoided the

strange and absurd beliefs of the former, and did not deny that the Lord was born of a virgin and of the Holy Spirit. But, nevertheless, inasmuch as they also refused to acknowledge that he pre-existed, being God, Word, and Wisdom, they turned aside into the impiety of the former, especially when they, like them, endeavored to observe strictly the bodily worship of the law. These men, moreover, thought that it was necessary to reject all the epistles of the apostle, whom they called an apostate from the law; andthey used only the so-called Gospel according to the Hebrews and made small account of the rest. The Sabbath and the rest of the discipline of the Jews they observed just like them, but at the same time, like us, they celebrated the Lord's days as a memorial of the resurrection of the Saviour. Wherefore, in consequence of such a course they received the name of Ebionites, which signified the poverty of their understanding. For this is the name by which a poor man is called among the Hebrews." EUSEBIUS Church History, Book 3, Chapter 27. GIBBON, Chapter 15.

7—Y
"For immediately, during the reign of Claudius, the all-good and gracious Providence, which watches over all things, led Peter, that strongest and greatest of the apostles, and the one who on account of his virtue was the speaker for all the others, to Rome against this great corrupter of life. (Simon Magus) He like a noble commander of God, clad in divine armor, carried the costly merchandise of the light of the understanding from the East to those who dwelt in the West, proclaiming the light itself, and the word which brings salvation to souls, and preaching the kingdom of Heaven." EUSEBIUS, Church History, Book 2, Chapter 14.

"The tradition that Peter suffered martyrdom in Rome is as old and as universal as that in regard to Paul but owing to a great amount of falsehood which became mixed with the original tradition by the end of the second century the whole has been rejected as untrue by some modern critics, who go so far as to deny that

Peter was ever at Rome." (Translator's note on Eusebius' Church History at Book 2, Chapter 25)

7—Z
"When expounding the first Psalm, he (Origen) gives a catalogue of the sacred Scriptures of the Old Testament as follows: 'It should be stated that the canonical books, as the Hebrews have handed them down, are twenty-two; corresponding with the number of their letters.' Further on he says: (The twenty two books of the Hebrews are the following: That which is called Genesis, but by the Hebrews, from the beginning of the book, Beresith, which means, in the beginning; Exodus, Welesmoth, that is, these are the names; Leviticus, Wikra, and he called; Numbers, Ammesphekodeim; Deuteronomy, Eleaddebareim, these are the words; Jesus (or Joshua) the son of Nave, Josoue ben Noun; Judges and Ruth, among them in one book, Saphateim; the First and Second of Kings, among them one. Samouel, that is, the called of God; the Third and Fourth of Kings in one, Wammelch David, that is, the Kingdom of David; of the Chronicles, the First and second in one, Dabreiamein, that is Records of days; Esdras, First and Second in one, Exra, (Meaning Ezra and Nehemiah), that is, an assistant; the book of Psalms, Spharthelleim; the Proverbs of Solomon, Moloth; Ecclesiastes, Koelth; the Sons of Songs (not, as some suppose, Songs of Songs), Sir Hassirim; Isaiah, Jessia, Jeremiah, with Lamentations and the epistle in one, Jeremiah; Daniel, Daniel; Ezekiel, Jezekiel; Job, Job; Esther, Esther. And besides these there are the Maccabees, which are entitled Snrbeth Sabanaiel. He gives these in the above-mentioned work. In his first book on Matthew's Gospel, maintaining the Canon of the Church, he testifies that, he knows only four Gospels, writing as follows: 'Among the four Gospels, which are the only indisputable ones in the Church of God under heaven, I have learned by tradition that the first was written by Matthew, who was once a publican, but afterwards an apostle of Jesus Christ, and it was prepared for the converts from Judaism, and published in the Hebrew language. The second is by

Mark, who composed it according to the instructions of Peter, who in his Catholic epistle acknowledges him as his son, saying, "The Church that is at Babylon elected together with you, saluteth you, and so doth, Marcus, my son. And the third by Luke, the Gospel commended by Paul, and composed for Gentile converts. Last of all that by John." EUSEBIUS, Church History, Book 6, Chapter 25. Quoted from Origen.

"Since we are dealing with this subject it is proper to sum up the writings of the New Testament which have been already-mentioned. First then must be put the holy quaternion of the Gospels; following them the Acts of the Apostles. After this must be reckoned the Epistles of Paul; next in order the extant former epistle of John, and likewise the epistle of Peter, must be maintained. After them is to be placed, if it really seems proper, the Apocalypse of John, concerning which we shall give the different opinions at a proper time. These then belong among the accepted writings. Among the disputed writings, which are nevertheless recognized by many, are extant the so-called epistle of James, and that, of Jude, also the second epistle of Peter, and those that are called the second and third of John, whether they belong to the evangelist or to another person of the same name. Among the rejected writings must be reckoned also the Acts of Paul, and the so-called Shepherd, and the Apocalypse of Peter, and in addition to these the extant epistle of Barabas, and the so-called Teachings of the Apostles; and besides, as I said, the Apocalypse of John, if it seem proper, which some, as I said, reject, but which others class with the accepted books. And among these some have placed also the Gospel according to the Hebrews, with which those of the Hebrews that have accepted Christ are especially delighted. And all these may be reckoned among the disputed books." EUSEBIUS, Church History, Book 3, Chapter 25.

8—A
"LINE OF KINGS—(Of Babylon) Nabopolassar, Nebuchadnezzar, Evil-merodach, Neriglissar, Laborosoarchod, or Labossora-

cus, Nabonadius the last king. Not being of royal birth, he married a daughter of Nebuchadnezzar (probably Neriglissar's widow), and as soon as his son by this marriage, Belshazzar (Belshar-uzur), is of sufficient age, associates him on the throne."—RAWLINSON, Ancient History, Page 49.

8—B
"Phoenicia, notwithstanding the small extent of its territory, which consisted of a mere strip of land between the crest of Lebanon and the sea, was one of the most important countries of the ancient world. In her the commercial spirit first showed itself as the dominant spirit of a nation. She was the carrier between the East and the West—the link that bound them together—in times anterior to the first appearance of the Greeks as navigators. The commercial spirit of Phoenicia was largely displayed during this period, which, till toward its close, was one of absolute independence. The great monarchies of Egypt and Assyria were now, comparatively speaking, weak; and the states between the Euphrates and the African border, being free from external control, were able to pursue their natural bent without interference. Her commercial leanings early induced Phoenicia to begin the practice of establishing colonies; and the advantages which the system was found to secure caused it to acquire speedily a vast development. The coasts and islands of the Mediterranean were rapidly covered with settlements; the Pillars of Hercules were passed, and cities built on the shores of the ocean. At the same time factories were established in the Persian Gulf; and, conjointly with the Jews, on the Red Sea. Phoenicia had at this time no serious commercial rival, and the trade of the world was in her hands."
RAWLINSON, Ancient History, pages 52, 54.

8—C
"According to the traditions of the Greeks, some important foreign elements were received into the nation during the period of which we are treating, Egyptians settled in Attica and Argolis; Phoenicians in Beotia; and Mysians, or Phrygians, at Argos. The

90 | *Historical Quotations*

civilization of the settlers was higher than that of the people among whom they settled, and some considerable benefits were obtained from these foreign sources. Among them may be especially mentioned letters, which were derived from the Phoenicians, probably anterior to B. C. 1100." RAWLINSON, Ancient History, page 139. HERODOTUS, 5-57.

8—D
"The 'Ahasuerus' of the Book of Esther has been identified by writers of repute with Daris Hystaspis, and with Artaxerxes Longimanus, as well as with Xerxes. But the notes of time, character, and name, which all point to Xerxes, have produced among modern a consensus in his favor. The historical character of the narrative is proved by the institution of the feats of Purim, which is still kept by the Jews, and of which no other account can be given." RAWLINSON, Ancient History, page 348.

8—E
"LINE OF JEWISH GOVERNORS form B. C. 37 to A. D. 44;— 1. Herod the Great. Obtains his crown by the favor of Antony, B. C. 37. Marries Mariamne, the Asmonaean princess, the same year. His dominions increased by Augustus, after Aetium, B. C. 30. Rebuilds the Temple with great magnificence, but also rebuilds that on Mt. Gerizim, and at Caesarea erects heathen temples. Maintains a body-guard of foreign mercenaries. Cruel and suspicious especially toward the members of his own family. Put to death Mariamne, her grandfather Hyrcanus, her two sons Aristobulus and Alexander, Antipater, his eldest son, and others. Dies B. C. 4 (according to the received chronology). 2. Archelaus; 3. Antipas; and 4. Philip, inherit portions of their father's dominions, Archelaus having Idumaea, Judea, and Samaria; Antipas, Galilee and Para, and Philip, Ituraea and Trachonitis. Archelaus rules oppressively, and is deposed by the Romans, A. D. 8, who add his dominions to the province of Syria, but assign the actual government to Procurators. These were: 5, Coponius; 6, M. Ambivius; 7, Annius Rufus; 8, Valerius Gratus, A. D. 14 to 25; 9,

Pontius Pilate, A. D. 25 to 36; 10, Marcellus. Antipas ruled in Galilee from B. C. 4 to A. D. 37, when he died. As these principalities became vacant they were conferred by the favor of Caligula on 11, Herod Agrippa the son of Aristobulus, who in A. D. 41 received from Claudius the further addition to his kingdom of Samaria and Judea, and thus united under his sway all Palestine. He died, after commencing a persecution of all Christians, A. D. 44; whereupon the Romans placed Palestine once more under the government of Procurators. Those in Judea were: 12, Caspius Radus, A. D. 44 to 48; 13, Ventidius Cumanus, A. II. 48 to 49; 14, Antionius Felix, A. D. 49 to 55; 15, Porcius Festus, A. D. 55 to 59; 16, Albinus, A. D. 62 to 65; and 17, Gessius Florus, under whom the Jews broke out into open rebellion. Paralell with this later line of Procurators was the government of Herod Agrippa II, first in Chaicis, and then in Abilene and Trachonitis, from A. D. 50 to 70, when his principality was swallowed up in the new arrangements consequent upon the revolt of the Jews and their reduction. Agrippa assisted the Romans in the Jewish War; and at its close retired to Rome, where he lived till the third year of Trajan, A. D. 100." RAWLINSON, Ancient History, page 355.

8—F
"According to the Hebrew text of Exod. 12:40, 41, a space of nearly four centuries and a half intervened between the entrance of the children of Israel into Egypt and their exodus under the leadership of Moses; and, although the real duration of the period is disputed, the balance of probability is in favor of this long term rather than of a shorter one. The growth of a tribe, numbering even three thousand persons, into a nation of above two millions, abnormal and remarkable if it took place within a period of four hundred and thirty years, would be still more strange and astonishing if the space of time were seriously curtailed. The ten generations between Jacob and Joshua (1 Chron. 7:22-27), who was a grown man at the time of the Exodus, require a term of four centuries rather than one or two. Egyptian chronology also

favors the longer period." RAWLINSON, Moses, His Life and Times, page 6.

8—G
"When Cyrus had avenged himself on the river Gyndes by distributing it into three hundred and sixty channels, and the second spring began to shine, he then advanced against Babylon. But the Babylonians having taken the field, awaited his coming; and when he had advanced near the city, the Babylonians gave battle, and, being defeated, were shut up in the city. But as they had been long aware of the restless spirit of Cyrus, and saw that he attacked all nations alike, they had laid up provisions for many years; and therefore, were under no apprehensions about a siege. On the other hand, Cyrus found himself in difficulty, since much time had elapsed, and his affairs were not at all advanced. Whether therefore some one else made the suggestion to him in his perplexity, or whether he himself devised the plan, he had recourse to the following stratagem. Having stationed the bulk of his army near the passage of the river where it enters Babylon, and again having stationed another division beyond the city, where the river makes its exit, he (gave orders to his forces to enter the city as soon as they should see the stream fordable. Having thus stationed his forces, and given these directions, he himself marched away with the ineffective part of his army; and having come to the lake, Cyrus did the same with respect to the river and lake as the queen of Babylonians had done. For having diverted the river by means of a canal, into the lake, which was before a swamp, he made the ancient channel fordable by the sinking of the river. When this took place, the Persians who were appointed to that purpose close to the stream of the river, which had not subsided to about the middle of a man's thigh, entered. Babylon by this passage. If, however, the Babylonians had been aware of it beforehand, or not known what Cyrus was about, they would not have suffered the Persians to enter the city, but would have utterly destroyed them; for having shut all the little gates that lead down to the river, they would have caught them as in a net; whereas the

Persians came upon them by surprise. It is related by the people who inhabited this city, that by reason of its great extent, when they who were at the extremities were taken, those of the Babylonians who inhabited the centre knew nothing of the capture; (for it happened to be a festival) but they were dancing at the time, and enjoying themselves, till they received certain information of the truth; and thus, Babylon was taken for the first time. HERODOTUS, 1-190-191.

"In his march to Babylon he (Cyrus) overthrew the Phrygians of the Greater Phrygia. He overthrew the Cappadocians, and he subjected the Arabians. And out of all these he armed no less than forty thousand horsemen. Abundance of the horse that belonged to prisoners taken, he distributed amongst all his allies. He came at last to Babylon, bringing with him a mighty multitude of horses, a mighty multitude of archers and javelin-men, but slingers innumerable.

"When Cyrus got to Babylon he posted his whole army around the city, then rode round the city himself, together with his friends, and with such of his allies as he thought proper. When he had taken a view of the walls he prepared for drawing off the army from before the city; and a certain deserter coming off, told him that they intended to fall on him when he drew off the army. Then Cyrus said: 'Crysantas, let us lay aside these things that are above our force; it is our business, as soon as possible, to dig as broad and as deep a ditch as we can, each part of us measuring out his proportion, that by this means we may want the fewer men to keep watch. So, measuring out the ground around the wall, and from the side of the river, leaving a space sufficient for large turrets, he dug round the wall on every side a very great ditch; and they threw up the earth towards themselves. In the first place, he built the turrets on the river, laying their foundation on palm-trees, that were not less than a hundred feet in length, for there are those of them that grew even to a greater length than that; and palm-treds, that are pressed, bent up under the weight as asses do that are used to the pack-saddle. He placed the turrets on these; for this reason, that it might carry the stronger appearance of his preparing to block up the city, and as if he intended that if the river made its way into the ditch it might not carry off the turrets. He raised likewise, a great many other turrets, on the rampart of earth, that he might have as many places as were proper for his watches. These people were thus employed. But they that were within the walls laughed at this blockade, as being themselves provided with necessaries for above twenty years. Cyrus hearing this, divided his army into twelve parts, as if he intended that each part should serve on the watch one month in the year. And when the Babylonians heard this they laughed yet more than before; thinking with themselves that they were to be watched by the Phrigians, Lydians, Arabians, and Cappadocians, men that were better affected to them than were to the Persians. The ditches were now finished. And Cyrus, when he heard that they were celebrating a festival in Babylon, in which all the Babylonians drank and reveled, the whole night; on that occasion, as soon as it grew dark, took a number of men with him, and opened the ditches into the river. When this was done the water ran off in the night by the ditches, and the passage of the river through the city became passable. When the affair of the river was thus managed Cyrus gave orders to the Persian commanders of thousands, both foot and horse, to attend him, each with his thousand drawn up two in front, and the rest of the allies to follow in the rear, ranged as they used to be before. They came accordingly. Then he making those that attended his person, both foot and horse, to go down into the dry part of the river, ordered them to try whether the channel of the river was passable. And when they brought him word that it was passable, he then called together the commanders, both of foot and horse, and spoke to them in this manner: 'The river, my friends, has yielded us a passage into the city; let us boldly enter, and not fear any thing within, considering that these people that we are now to march against are the same that we defeated while they had their allies attending them, while they were awake, sober, armed, and in order. But now we march to them at a time that many of them are asleep, many drunk, and all of them in confusion, and when they discover that we are got in, they will then, by means of their consternation, be yet more unfit for service than they are now.' When this was said they marched; and, of course that they met with some they fell on and killed, some fled, and some set up a clamor. They that were with Gobryas joined in the clamor with them, as if they were revelers themselves, and marching on the shortest way that they could, they got round about the place. . . . As soon as the noise and clamor began, they that were within perceiving the disturbance, and the king commanding them to examine what the matter was, ran out throwing open the gates. They that were with Gadatas, as soon as they saw the gates loose, broke in, pressing forward on the runaways and dealing their blows amongst them, they came up to the king, and found him now in a standing posture, with his sword drawn. They that were with Gadatas and Gobryas, being many in number, mastered him." XENOPHON, Cyclopedia, Book 7, Chapters 4 and 5. RAWLINSON, Five Great Monarchies, Vol. 3, pages 70, 72.

8—H
"After this he entered the royal palace and, they that conveyed the treasures from Sardis delivered them up here. When Cyrus entered, he first sacrificed to the goddess Vesta, and then to Regal Jone, and to whatever other deity the magi thought proper. Having done this, he now began to regulate other affairs; and considering what his business was, and that he was taking on him the government of great multitudes of men, he prepared to take up his habitation in the greatest city of all that were of note in the world, and this city had as great enmity to him as any city could have to a man." XENOPHON, Cyclopedia, Book 7, Chapter 5.

8—I
"After he (Cyrus the Younger) had left the mountains, he advanced through the plain, and having made five and twenty parasangs in four days' march, arrived at Tarsus, a large and rich

city of Cilicia, where stood the palace of Syennesis, king of Cilicia; having the river Cydnus running through the middle of it, and is two hundred feet in breadth." XENOPHON, Anabasis, Book 1, Chapter 2.

8—J
"Final division of the Empire (A. D. 395).—The Roman world was united practically for the last time under Theodosius the Great. From A. D. 392 to 395 he ruled as sole emperor. Just before his death he divided the empire between his two sons, Arcadius and Honoring, assigning the former, who was only eighteen years of age, the government of the East, and giving the latter, a mere child of eleven, the sovereignty of the West. This division was not to affect the unity of the empire. There was to be but one empire, although there were to be two emperors. But as a matter of fact, so different was the course of events in the two halves of the old empire that from this on we shall find it convenient to trace the history of each division separately." MYERS, Ancient History, p. 536.

"Theodosius, therefore, had no sooner defeated Eugenius, than he sent for his younger son, Honorius, a boy of eleven, and prepared to make over to him the Western Empire. Soon afterwards, finding his end approaching, he formally divided his dominions between his two sons, leaving the East to Arcadius, the elder, and the West to Honorius, whom he placed under the guardianship of the general Stilicho, Theodosius expired at Milan in the fiftieth year of his age and the sixteenth of his reign, January 17, A. D. 395. . . . Hitherto the East and West, if politically separate governments, had been united by sympathy, by the mutual lending and receiving of assistance, and by the idea, at any rate, that in some sense they formed one empire. With Arcadius and Honorius this idea begins to fade and disappear; relations of friendship between the governments are replaced by feelings of jealousy, of mutual repulsion, of suspicion, distrust, and dislike. Hence the disruption of the empire is ordinarily dated from this time, though the separation was really so gradual that the historian acts somewhat arbitrarily in fixing on any definite point. There is, however, none better than the date commonly taken; and, as the Eastern or Byzantine Empire belongs confessedly to Modern and not to Ancient History, the fortunes of the Western Empire will alone be followed in this concluding section of the history of Ancient Rome. The origin of the estrangement between the East and West appears to have been the mutual jealousy and conflicting pretentions of Ruflnus, the minister of the Eastern, and St. Hicho, the general and guardian of the Western emperor." RAWLINSON, Ancient History, pages 595, 596.

8—K
"No two churches are so much alike in their creed, policy and cultus, as the Greek and Roman; and yet no two are such irreconcilable rivals, perhaps for the very reason of their affinity. They agree much more than either agrees with any Protestant church. They were never organically united. They differed from the beginning in nationality, language, and genius, as the ancient Greeks differed from the Romans; yet they grew up together, and stood shoulder to shoulder in the ancient conflict with Paganism and heresy. They co-operated in the early ecumenical councils, and adopted their doctrinal and ritual decisions. But the development of the papal Monarchy, and the establishment of a Western Empire in connection with it, laid the foundation of a schism which has not been healed to this day. The controversy culminated in the rivalry between the patriarch of Constantinople and the Pope of Rome. It first broke out under Photius and Nichilas I, who excommunicated each other (869 and 879). Photius, the greatest scholar of his age, whom Pope Nicolas refused to acknowledge as patriarch, charged, in a. famous encyclical letter, the Roman Church with heresy, for the unauthorized insertion of the Filioque into the Nicene Creed, and with various corrupting practices. The controversy was renewed under the Patriarch Cerularius (1053) and became irreconcilable through the Venetian conquest of Constantinople (1204), and the establishment of a

98 | *Historical Quotations*

Latin Empire (1204-61), and Latin rival bishoprics in eastern seas, with the sanction of Pope Innocent III. Attempts at a re-union were made from time to time, especially in the Council of Lyons (1274) and the Council of Ferrara (1439) but all in vain. The compromise formula of the latter council was rejected with scorn in the East, as treason to the orthodox faith. With the fall of Constantinople (1453) the political motive for seeking a union with the West ceased; and the schism continues to this day, even with increased force, since the Vatican Council in 1870 intensified the chief cause of separation by declaring papal absolutism and papal infallibility an article of faith. Popery knows no compromise; and the Greek Church can never submit to its authority without committing suicide.

"The points in which the Greek Church differs from the Roman are the following; the single procession of the Holy Spirit (against the Filioque); the equality of the patriarchs, and the rejection of the papacy as an antichristian innovation and usurpation; the right of the lower clergy (priests and deacons) to marry (though only one); the communion under both kinds (against the withdrawal of the cup from the laity); trine immersion as the only valid form of baptism; the use of the vernacular languages in worship; a number of minor ceremonies, as the use of common or leavened bread in the Eucharist, infant communion, the repetition of holy union (euxelaion) in sickness, etc." SCHAFF-HERZOG ENCYCLOPEDIA, Article—Greek Church. See also MOSHEIM, 4-S-2-7, 8.

8—L
"The word 'Pope' is the Latin papa, from the Greek PAPPAS, and means 'father.' It was anciently given to all Christian teachers, then to all bishops and abbots, then limited to the Bishop of Rome -and the Patriarchs of Alexander, Antioch, Jerusalem and Constantinople. In the Greek Church to-day it is the customary address of every secular priest. The name appears, as first applied to the Bishop of Rome, in the letter of a deacon, Severus, to Mar-

cellinus (296-304); was first formally adopted by Siricius (Bishop of Rome from 384 to 398), in his Epist. and Orthod. prov.; officially used since Leo. I. (440-461); and declared the exclusive right of the papacy by the decree of Gregory VII. (1073-85)." SCHAFF-HERZOG ENCY, Art. POPE.

"Whoever, therefore, compares these particulars, will easily perceive that the only dignity which the Bishop of Rome could justly claim was a preeminence of order and association, not of power and authority. Or to explain the matter yet more clearly, the preeminence of the bishop of Rome, in the universal church, was such as that of Cyprian, bishop of Carthage, was in the African churches. 'If, indeed, we are to give credit to Anastasius and Paul the Deacon, something like what we have now related was transacted by Phocas: for, when the bishops of Constantinople maintained that their church was not only equal in dignity and authority to that of Rome, but also the head of all the Christian churches, this tyrant opposed their pretentions, and granted the pre-eminence to the church of Rome: and thus was the papal supremacy first introduced." MOSHEIM, Cen. 3, p. 2, Chap. 2 and Cen. 7, page 2, Chapter 2.

"We observe that already, in early times, there were traces in the Romish bishops of an assumption, that a peculiarly decisive authority was due to them, as the successors of St. Peter, in Church controversies, and that the 'cathedra Petri' was to have a prevailing sway before all other 'ecclesiae apostolieac,' as the source of apostolic tradition. The Romish bishop Victor, gave a specimen of this assumption, when he excommunicated the churches of Asia Minor, about A. D. 190, in consequence of a trifling dispute about a mere external point." NEANDER, Church History, page 125. "Pope. 5. Eccl. Hist. a. In the early church, a bishop, b, In the Eastern Church, the bishop or patriarch of Alexandria. He (Alexander, Bishop of Alexandria) was known by a tile which he alone officially bore in the assembly (Council of Nicaea). He was 'the Pope,. 'The Pope of Rome' was a phrase which had not yet emerged in history. But 'Pope of Alexandria' was a well-known dignity. A. P. Stanley." WEBSTER'S NEW INTERNATIONAL DICTIONARY.

8—M
"And those ministers of the gods, whom they employ to execute their bidding, remain to us invisible; for, though the thunderbolt is shot from on high, and breaketh in pieces whatever it findeth in its way, yet no one seeth it when it falls, when it strikes, or when it retires; neither are the winds discoverable to our sight, though we plainly behold the ravages that everywhere make; and With ease perceive what time they are rising. And if there be any thing in man, my Euthedemus, partaking of the divine nature, it must surely be the soul which governs and directs him; yet no one considers this an object of his sight. Learn, therefore, not to despise those things which ye cannot see; judge of the greatness of the power by the effects which are produced, and REVERENCE THE DEITY." Words of Socrates in XENOPHON, Memoirs of Socrates, Book 4, Chapter 3.

8—N
"The whole nation of the Gauls is extremely addicted to superstition: whence, in threatening distempers, and the imminent dangers of war, they make no scruple to sacrifice men, or engage themselves by vow to such sacrifices; in which they make use of the ministry of the Druids: for it is a prevalent opinion among them, that nothing but the life of man can atone for the life of man; insomuch that they have established even public sacrifices of this kind. Some prepare huge Colossusses, of osier twigs, into which they put men alive, and setting fire to them, those within expire amidst the flames. They prefer for victims such as have been convicted of theft, robbery, or other crimes; believing them the most acceptable to the gods: but when real criminals are wanting, the innocent are often made to suffer." CAESAR, Commentaries, Book VI, Chapter XV.

8—O
"When it is asked, to whom do we owe the canon? the usual answer is, to the Church, which is hardly correct. The Church Catholic did not exist till after the middle of the second century. The preservation of the early Christian writings was owing, in the first instance, to the congregations to whom they were sent, and the neighboring ones with whom such congregations had friendly connection. The care of them devolved on the most influential teachers—on those who occupied leading positions in the chief cities, or were most interested in apostolic writings as a source of instruction. The Christian books were mostly in the hands of the bishops. In process of time the canon was the care of assemblies or councils. But it had been made before the first general by a few leading fathers toward the end of the second century in different countries. The formation of a Catholic Church and of a canon was simultaneous. The circumstances in which the collection originated was unfavorable to the authenticity of its materials, for tradition had been busy over them and their authors. Instead of attributing the formation of the canon to the Church, it would be more correct to say that the important stage in it was due to three teachers, each working separately and in his own way, who were intent upon the creation of a Christian society which did not appear in the apostolic age, a visible organization united in faith—where the discordant opinions of apostolic and sub-apostolic times should be finally merged. The canon was not the work of the Christian Church so much as of the men who were striving to form the Church, and could not get beyond the mould received by primitive 'Christian literature.' The first mention of a 'Catholic Church' occurs in The Martyrdom of Polycarp, an epistle that cannot be dated earlier than 160 A. D., and may perhaps be ten years later. But though the idea be there and in the Ignatian epistles, its established use is due to Irenaeus, Tertullian, and Cyprian." ENCYCLOPAEDIA BRITTANNICA, Vol. 1, Article—CANON.

102 | *Historical Quotations*

8—P
"ADVENTISTS, or the followers of William Miller, a fanatical student of prophecy, who put the second advent of Christ in the year 1843. The sect arose in New England in 1833, and once numbered, it is said, fifty thousand persons; but now, owing to the repeated failures to get the right date for the event, it has dwindled into much smaller proportions. The 'Seventh Day Adventists,' as they now are called, do not pretend to foretell the exact day of Christ's coming; but they keep the event continually before them. They practice immersion; believe in the annihilation of the wicked, and in the sleep of the soul from the hour of death to the day of judgment." "ADVENTIST, the general name of a body, embracing several branches, who look for the proximate coming of Christ. . . The oldest branch is the Evangelical Adventists. They believe in the natural immortality of the soul and in eternal future punishment. . . They publish a weekly paper in Boston, called Messiah's Herald. Their number has been estimated at from 5,000 to 9,000. The third branch, the Seventh-Day Adventists, has a compacted organization, and has grown considerably, especially in the West. Its headquarters are at Battle Creek, Mich., where it has a health institution, a college, a publishing house, and other denominational enterprises. It maintains a number of missionaries abroad, and does home missionary work very systematically. It holds that it is still obligatory to observe the seventh day' as the sabbath, and believes in visions as seen by Mrs. White, who has published several volumes of visions and testimonies. It numbers 16,000 or 17,000."

SCHAFF HERZOG ENCYCLOPAEDIA. Article—Adventists. Encyclopaedia Britannica, Vol. 25, page 52.

8—Q
"HISTORY, Baptists in Europe—The early Baptists of the continent of Europe held the same evangelical truths, and the same view of the church, as the later Baptists of England and America; but they differed from these latter in many other points. The Bap-

tists appeared first in Switzerland, about A. D. 1523, where they were persecuted by Zwingli and the Romanists. . . Baptists in America—In America the earliest Baptists were found in the Massachusetts Colony, but were driven out. Some went to Rhode Island, and others to New York and Virginia, in 1770, so far as is known, the Baptists numbered 77 churches with about 5,000 members in the colonies." SCHAFF-HERZOG ENCYCLOPAEDIA, Article—Baptists.

8—R
"MENNONITES is a name borne by certain Christian communities in Europe and America, denoting their adherance to a type of doctrine of which Menno Simons was, not indeed the originator, but the chief exponent at the time when the anti-paedo-baptism of the congregations which he labored took permanent form in opposition to ordinary Protestantism on the one hand and to the theocratic ideas of the Munster type of anabaptism on the other. The original home of the views afterward called Mennonite was in Zurich, where, as early as 1525, Grebel and Manz founded a community having for its most distinctive mark baptism upon confession of faith." ENCYCLOPAEDIA BRITANNICA, Vol. 16, Article—Mennonites. SCHAFF-HERZOG ENCYCLOPAEDIA, Article—Mennonites.

8—S
"Joseph Smith, the founder of the Mormon sect, was born in Sharon, Windsor County, Vt., Dec. 23, 1805. He had six brothers and three sisters. In 1815 his father moved to Palmyra, and afterward to Manchester, contiguous towns in Ontario (now Wayne) County, N. Y. In 1820 an unusual religious excitement prevailed in Manchester and the region round about. Five of the Smith family' were awakened, and united with the Presbyterians. Joseph, in his own account of his early life, says he 'became somewhat partial to the Methodist sect.' He says he prayed to be guided aright; and that finally' two heavenly messengers bade him not to join any sect, and, three years afterwards, another celestial

visitant outlined to him about the golden plates he was to find, and the prophet he was to be. This was on Sept. 22, 1823; and from this time on, he avers, his days and nights were filled, and his life was guided, by 'visions,' 'voices,' and 'angels.' The hill Cumorah was about four miles from Palmyra, between that town and Manchester. Here, in the fall of 1827, he claims he exhumed the golden plates. For more than two years, by the aid of the 'Urim and Thummim' found with them, he was engaged in translating their contents into English. In March, 1830, the translation was given into the printer's hands. This is his history of himself. . . . While digging for treasure at Harmony, Penn., he boarded in the house of Mr. Isaac Hale. On the 18th of January, 1827, he married the daughter, Emma Hale, much against her father's wishes, having been compelled to take her away from her home for the wedding. In 1828, Martin Harris, a farmer of Palmyra, was amanuensis for him. In 1829 Oliver Cowdery, a school teacher of the neighborhood, filled the same office. On May 15, 1829, by command of an angelic messenger calling himself John the Baptist, Smith baptized Cowdery, and then Cowdery baptized him. Afterward he ordained Cowdery to the Aaronic priesthood, and Cowdery ordained him. And, in process of time, it is claimed, Smith received the Melchisedec priesthood at the hands of the apostles Peter, James and John. Some of the prophet's family, and some of a family named Whitmer, in Fayette, Seneca County, N. Y., became converts; and on April 6, 1830, in Whitmer's house the Mormon 'Church' began its history. That day it was organized, with a membership of six—the prophet and two of his brothers, two Whitmers and Oliver Cowdery. Within a week or two the first miracle of the 'new dispensation' was wrought; the prophet casting out a devil from Newell Knight of Colesville, Broome County, N. Y., whose vissage and limbs were frightfully distorted by the demoniacal possession. In December, 1830, Sidney Rigdon, a Campbellite preacher in Ohio, became a convert. Rigdon was erratic, but eloquent; self-opinionated, but well versed in the Scriptures; and in literary culture and intellectual force was the greatest man among the early Mormons. He was born in Pennsylvania, and was twelve years older than Smith. Thereafter the new sect strengthened and spread. . . SCHISMS. One only that is of any considerable importance now exists, known as the 'Josephites.' The Josephites are so called after Joseph Smith, the son of the prophet, their chief. They call themselves the 'Re-organized Church of Jesus Christ of Latter-Day Saints.' They had headquarters at Plano, Ill., and maintain a few preachers in Utah, who do not, however, make much headway. They repudiate polygamy 'say that the prophet never taught it,' brand Brigham as a usurper, and claim that Smith the son is the rightful successor of the father in the leadership of the church."

SCHAFF-HERZOG ENCYCLOPAEDIA, Article—Mormons.

"MORMONS—Church organized, 1830; Nauvoo founded, 1840; expelled from Nauvoo, 1846; migration to the Great Salt Lake, 1848, Rebellion, 1857-'8." HISTORICAL REFERENCE BOOK, by Louis Heil prin. ENCYCLOPAEDIA BRITANNICA, Vol. 16, Article—Mormons.

8—T
"The Universalist denomination traces its origin directly to James Belly, a London, preacher in the middle and last part of the eighteenth century, who wrote a book called The Union, and who had for his disciple John Murray. The latter came to this country in September, 1770, and immediately began preaching at various places along the Atlantic seaboard, from New Jersey to Massachusetts, establishing himself at Gloucester four years later. Through the efforts of Mr. Murray, and a few who entertained similar views, churches were established at important points in the New England and Middle States. But the doctrine spread somewhat slowly. In the year 1800, there were scarcely more than twenty Universalist ministers in the country. At that time the Reb.

Hosea Ballou, who is justly called the father of Universalism in its present form, was approaching the maturity of his powers."

    SCHAFF1HERZOG ENCYCLOPAEDIA. Article—Universalism.
    ENCYCLOPAEDIA BRITTANNICA, Article—Universalist, Church.

8—U
"PROTESTANT EPISCOPAL CHURCH. In the United States of America, the legal title of that offshoot of the Church of England that was organized in the United States after the achievement of their independence. The expression Protestant Episcopal came into vogue in Maryland during the Revolution War. At that time the title Church of England, which this religious body had borne during colonial times, if it had not become a misnomer, was prejudicial in the minds of a nation striving to throw off the British yoke. The name that came into use indicates that this church is protestant toward the Church of Rome, and episcopal among Protestants. In 1789 a general convention of all dioceses fixed this title, and it has remained unchanged, notwithstanding repeated proposals by Ritualists and High Churchmen to take a name of vaster comprehension." ENCYCLOPAEDIA BRITTANNICA. Article—Protestant Episcopal Church.

"EPISCOPAL CHURCH—The first known clerical representative of the Church of England in America was Albert de Prato, a learned mathematician, and a canon of St. Paul's, London, who visited St. John's, Newfoundland in August, 1527. The next clergyman appeared after the Reformation, in connection with Frobisher's expedition of 1578. This was Woolfall, who landed in the Countess of Warwick's Sound, and celebrated the first English communion recorded in connection with the New World. . . . The doctrine of the church, as drawn from Holy Scripture, is incorporated in the Book of Common Prayer, and is expressed chiefly by means of the Apostles' and the Nicene Creed, together with thirty-eight of the Articles of the Church of England, modified to meet the condition of things in this country." SCHAFF-HERZOG ENCYCLOPAEDIA. Article—Episcopal Church.

8—V
"POURING. The pouring of water on the head is the usual act of baptism in the Church of Rome and the Protestant communions. Sometimes, especially in Protestant circles, a mere sprinkling is used, or a simple touching of the forehead with the moistened finger. What is the origin of the custom?

In the Apostolic Church the regular baptism was by immersion. The oldest undisputed mention of pouring is found in the Epistle of Cyprian to Magnus, about 250 A. D. Certain ones converted in sickness when immersion was out of the question, had received merely' a pouring (non loti, sed perfusi); and it was denied that they were Christians in good and regular standing (legitimate Christiani). . . For a long time pouring was considered as of but doubtful propriety. Those who received it were termed clinics, as having received only an irregular, or sick-bed baptism, and they were denied admission to the higher offices of the church. Yet there were exceptions. Novation, who 'had received only clinical baptism, was ordained presbyter in Rome, and was even the candidate of a party to the papal chair. Immersion still remains the usage of the Greek Church: and says Stanley, 'the most illustrious and venerable portion of it, that of the Byzantine Empire, absolutely repudiates and ignores any other mode of administration as essentially invalid.' It long remained the ordinary usage of the Church of Rome." SCHAFF-HERZOG. Vol. 3, p. 1876. Article—POURING.

EUSEBIUS, Book 6, Chapter 43.

8—W
"It is certain that Christ did not ordain infant baptism; he left, indeed, much, which was not needful for salvation, to the free

development of the Christian spirit, without here appointing binding laws. We cannot prove that the apostles ordained infant baptism. . . But immediately after Irenaeus, in the latter years of the second century, Tertullian appeared as a zealous opponent of infant baptism, a proof that it was not then usually considered as an apostolic ordinance, for in that case he would hardly have ventured to speak so strongly against it." NEANDER, Church History, 1st 3 Centuries, p. 198.

"No time can be assigned to the beginning of the practice of infant baptism. If it had been an innovation, it would have created a revolution, or at all events provoked a violent protest. But it gained ground gradually from the very beginning, as Christianity took hold of family life and training. Origen speaks of it as apostolic, and was himself baptized in infancy (about 180). . . . It must be admitted that adult baptism was the rule, infant baptism the exception, in the apostolic age, and continued to be till the church was fairly established in the Roman Empire." SCHAFF-HERZOG, Vol. 1, p. 210. Article—Baptism.

8—X
"As now the congregations grew larger, the social differences between the members began to make themselves felt, and the agapae changed character. They became entertainments of the rich. In Alexandria 'the psalms and hymns and spiritual songs' of old (Eph. 5:19) (Col. 3:16) were supplanted by performances on the lyre, the harp, and the flute, in spite of Clement's protest." SCHAFF-HERZOG, Vol. 1, p. 34. Article—AGAPE.

"The organ is said to have been first introduced into church music by Pope Vitalian I, in 666. In 757 a great organ was sent as a present to Pepin by the Byzantine Emperor, Constantine Copronyinus, and placed in the church of St. Corneille at Compiegne." CHAMBERS' ENCYCLOPAEDIA. Article—Organ.

8—Y
"SABBATH-DAY'S JOURNEY (Acts 1:12). From the injunction in Ex. 16:29 the scribes laid down the rule that an Israelite must not go two thousand yards beyond the limits of his abode. The permitted distance seems to have been grounded on the space to be kept between, the ark and the people (Josh. 3:4) in the wilderness, which tradition said was that between the ark and the tents. Whilst the rabbis on the one hand regulated the walking on the sabbath days by allowing only a certain space, yet on the other hand they also contrived certain means whereby the sabbath-day's walk could be exceeded, without transgressing the law, by the so-called mixtio terminorum, or connection of distances. They ordained that all those who wished to join their social gatherings on the sabbath were to deposit on Friday afternoon some article of food in a certain place at the end of the sabbath day's journey that it might thereby be constituted a domicile, and thus another sabbath-day's journey could be undertaken from the first terminus." SCHAFF-HERZOG, Vol. 3, p. 2089. Article—Sabbath-Day's Journey.

8—Z
"MODERN SUNDAY SCHOOLS—Sunday schools like those just noted were sporadic; there was need for a popular and general movement, bringing them into affiliation with each other, if not into an organized system. Of this great movement, Robert Raikes is justly regarded as the founder. He was a citizen of Gloucester, England, and proprietor of the Gloucester Journal. Business calling him into the suburbs of the city in 1780, where many youth were employed in the pin and other factories, his heart was touched by the groups of ragged, wretched, and cursing children. He engaged four female teachers, to receive and instruct in reading and in the Catechism such children as should be sent to them on Sunday. The children were required to come with clean hands and faces, and hair combed, and with such clothing as they had. They were to stay from ten to twelve, then to go home; to return at one, and after a lesson to be conducted to

church; after church to repeat portions of the Catechism; to go home at five quietly, without playing in the streets. Diligent scholars received rewards of Bibles, Testaments, books, combs, shoes, and clothing. The teachers were paid a shilling a day." SCHAFF-HERZOG, Vol. 3, p. 2262. Art., Sunday Schools. ENCYCLOPAEDIA BRITTANNICA, Article—Raikes, Robert.

9—A
"SALVATION ARMY, The—is a body of men and women, joined together after a fashion of an army, with a general, colonels, majors, captains, and lower officers, under whom are the privates, bent, as they claim, upon presenting the gospel in a manner to attract the attention of the lowest classed. Its organizer and leader is William Booth, by baptism a member of the Church of England, and by conversion a Wesleyan, and afterwards a minister of the Methodist New Connection. In this latter capacity he had great success; but in 1861 he withdrew from the regular ministry, and devoted himself to independent evangelistic work. In 1865 he came to the east of London, and there began the movement which resulted in the organization of the 'Salvation Army' in 1876." SCHAFF-HERZOG, Vol. 3, p. 2099. Article—Salvation Army.

9—B
"I. H. S., an inscription dating far back in the history of the Christian Church, but whose interpretation is somewhat doubtful. Some explain it as In Hoc Signo, scilicet, vinces ("with this token thou shalt be victorious"), the words accompanying the vision of the radiant cross appearing to Constantine and his army; others, as Jesus Hominum Salvator ("Jesus, Men's Saviour"), the motto of the Jesuits. The most probable explanation, however, is that which derives the inscription simply from the Greek IHSOYS ("Jesus"), as the transformation of the 8 into the Latin S presents no difficulties." SCHAFF- HERZOG, Vol. 2, p. 1061. Article—I. H. S.

"IHS. A symbol or monogram representing the Greek IHS, contraction of IHCSOV, Jesus. It is also written IHC, the variant form C (lunar sigma) taking the place of S. Other forms are: IHC, JHS, etc. In ignorance of its origin, the symbol is often regarded as an abbreviation of the Latin phrase Iesus Hominum Salvator, Jesus Saviour of Men, or of In Hoc Signo (Vinces), in this sign (thou shalt conquer), etc. WEBSTER'S NEW INTERNATIONAL DICTIONARY.

9—C
"I. N. R. I. Abbr. Iesus (Jesus) Nazarenus, Rex Iedaeorum (Judaeorum), (L. Jesus of Nazareth, King of the Jews). WEBSTER'S NEW INTERNATIONAL DICTIONARY, lower section.

9—D
"Protestant, (a) Originally, one of those German princes who, professing reformed doctrine, signed at the Diet of Spires on April 20 1529, a protest against the annulment of the decree of the Diet of Spires in 1526, which had been unanimously passed, calling upon the emperor to summon a general council, and meanwhile allowing each prince to manage the religious affairs of his territory as he saw fit." WEBSTER'S NEW INTERNATIONAL DICTIONARY.

"But the tranquility and liberty they enjoyed, in consequence of the resolutions taken in the first diet of Spires, were not of long duration. They were interrupted by a new diet assembled, in 1529, in the same place, by the emperor, after he had appeased the commotions and troubles which had employed his attention in several parts of Europe, and concluded a treaty of peace with Clement. This prince, having now, in a great measure, shaken off the burden that had for some time overwhelmed him, had leisure to direct the affairs of the church, and this the reformers soon felt by a disagreeable experience. For the power, which had been granted by the former diet to every prince of managing ecclesiastical matters as he thought proper, until the meeting of a general council, was new revoked by a majority of votes, and not only so, but every change was declared unlawful that should be introduced into the doctrine, discipline or worship of the established religion, before the determination of the approaching council was known. This decree was justly considered as iniquitous and intolerable by the elector of Saxony, the landgrave of Hesse, and such other members of the diet, as were persuaded of the necessity of a reformation in the church. Nor was any one so simple, or so little acquainted with the politics of Rome, as to look upon the promise of assembling speedily a general council, in any other light than as an artifice to quiet the minds of the people; since it was easy to perceive, that a lawful council, free from the despotic influence of Rome, was the very last thing that a pope would grant in such a critical state of affairs. Therefore, when the princes and the members above mentioned found that all their arguments and remonstrances against this unjust decree made no impression upon Ferdinand, (who was presiding while his brother, the emperor, was at Barcelona) or upon the abettors of the ancient superstitions, (whom the pope's legate animated by his presence and exhortations,) they entered a solemn protest against this decree, on the 19th of April, and appealed to the emperor and to a future council. Hence the denomination of Protestants, given from this period to those who renounce the superstitious communion of the church of Rome.

"The princes of the empire, who entered this protest, and are consequently to be considered as the first protestant princes, were John, elector of Saxony, George, elector of Brandenburg, for Franconia, Earnest and Francis, dukes of Lunenburg, the landgrave of Hesse, and the prince of Anhalt. These princes were supported by thirteen imperial towns, viz, Strasburg, Ulm, Nuremberg, Constance, Rottingen, Windsheim, Memmingen, Nordlingen, Lindaw, Kempten, Heilbron, Weissenburg, and St. Gall." MOSHEIM, Reformation, Cen. 16, Section 1, Chap. 2, Paragraph 26, and footnote.

9—E
"The Massacre of Saint Bartholomew's Day (August 25, 1572). Before the festivities which followed the nuptial ceremonies were over. (This was the marriage between Princess Margaret, sister of Charles IX, and Henry of Bourbon, the young king of Navarre, which was brought about by Catherine de Medici, mother of Charles IX. Her motive for this marriage was to cement the treaty of Saint-German which was favorable to the Huguenots. By the union of these two, the former of whom was Catholic and the latter Protestant, she thought the treaty would be strengthened.) The world was shocked by one of the most awful crimes recorded by history—the massacre of the Huguenots in Paris on Saint Bartholomew's Day.

"The circumstances which led to this fearful tragedy were as follows: Among the Protestant nobles who came up to Paris to attend the wedding was Admiral Coligny, (champion of the Protestants). The admiral had great influence over the young king, and this influence he used to draw him away from the queen mother and the Guises. Fearing the loss of her influence over her son (King Charles IX) Catherine resolved upon the death of the admiral. The attempt miscarried, Coligny receiving only a Slight wound from the assassin's ball.

"The Huguenots rallied about their wounded chief with loud threats of revenge. Catherine, driven on by insane fear, now determined Upon the death of all the Huguenots in Paris as the only measure of safety. By the 23rd of August, the plans for the massacre were all arranged. On the evening of that day, Catherine went to her son and represented to him that the Huguenots had formed a plot for the assassination of the royal family and the leaders of the Catholic party, and that the utter ruin of their house and cause could be averted only by the immediate destruction of the Protestants within the city walls. The order for the massacre was then laid before him for his signature. The weak-minded king shrank in terror from the deed, and at first refused to sign the decree; but overcome at last, by the representations of his mother, he exclaimed, 'I consent, provided not one Huguenot be left alive in France to reproach me with the deed.'

"A little past the hour of midnight on Saint Bartholomew's day (August 25, 1572), at a preconcerted signal (the tolling of a bell) the massacre began. Coligny was one of the first victims. After his assassins had done their work, they tossed the body out of the window of the chamber in which It lay into the street, in order that Henry, third Duke of Guise, who stood below, might satisfy himself that his enemy was really dead.

"For three days and nights the orgy of death went on within the city. All who were suspected of sympathizing with the reformers were killed without mercy. King Charles himself is said to have joined in the work, and to have fired upon the Huguenots from one of the windows of the Palace of the Louvre as they fled past. The number of victims in Paris is variously estimated at from one thousand to ten thousand. The dead bodies were dragged through the streets and flung into the Seine.

"With the capitol cleared of Huguenots, orders were issued to the principal cities of France to purge themselves in like manner of heretics. In many places the instincts of humanity prevailed over fear of the royal resentment, and the decree was disobeyed; but in other places the orders were carried out, and frightful massacres took place. The number of victims throughout the country is unknown; estimates differ widely, running from two thousand to a hundred thousand.

"The massacre of Saint Bartholomew's Day raised a cry of execration in every part of the civilized world, save at Rome and in Spain. Queen Elizabeth put her court in mourning, and her council denounced the slaughter as 'the most heinous act that had occurred in the world since the crucifixion of Jesus Christ.'

"The Protesting in the Netherlands, who, in their struggle with Philip, had been entertaining hopes of help from their French brethren, were plunged almost into despair at the unexpected and awful blow.

"On the other hand, Philip, when the news reached him, 'seemed more delighted than with all the good fortune or happy incidents which had ever before occurred to him,' and for the first time in his life the taciturn schemer is said to have laughed aloud; while at Rome, Pope Gregory XIII, believing that there had been a Huguenot conspiracy against the king from which he had saved himself by the massacre, returned public thanks to God for his manifest favor to the holy church, causing a Te Deum in commemoration of the event to be performed in the church of St. Mar. He also had a medal struck, bearing on one side his own effigy, and on the other a picture of a destroying angel slaying the Huguenots.

"Charles, who lived not quite two years after the massacre, suffered the keenest remorse for the part he had taken in the awful tragedy." THE MODERN AGE. Myers, 1904 Edition, pages 166-168.

9—F
"Of the successors of Augustus, the first, and by far the ablest, was his stepson, Tiberius. His merits as a soldier and administrator were well known to Augustus, who, even during his own lifetime, granted Tiberius a share in the government." WEBSTER, Ancient History, p. 447.

9—G
"The Society of Friends was founded during a period of intense religious enthusiasm in England, about 1850, under the leadership of George Fox." (From inscription on board on fence around Friends Church house, Philadelphia.

9—H
"Nothing was done for the regulation of the stream of the Tiber; excepting that they caused the only bridge, with which they still made shift (111.486), to be constructed of stone at least as far as the Tiber-island. As little was anything done toward the leveling of the city on the seven hills, except where perhaps the accumulation of rubbish had effected some improvement." MOMMSEN, History of Rome, Book 5, Chapter 11. INGE, Society in Rome Under Caesars, p. 247.

9—I
"But the people of the church in Jerusalem had been commanded by a revelation, vouchsafed to approved men there before the war, to leave the city and to dwell in a certain town of Perea called Pella." EUSEBIUS, Chapter 5, and note.

> MILLMAN, note on Gibbon's statement. Chap. 15, after note 18.
> YONGE, Young Folk's History. Rom., p. 306.

9—J
"And the ancient Romans further agreed with the Cretans and Laconians in taking their meals not, as was afterwards the custom among both peoples, in a reclining, but in a sitting posture." MOMMSEN, Book 1, Chapter 2.

"The custom of reclining, with the left elbow resting on a cushion, was now (in the days of the Caesars) universal for men; women and children sat, the position being considered more proper. This, however, like most customs founded on modesty, was often transgressed in our (period of the Caesars) period. Round tables, called stigmata, were sometimes used in imperial times, and couches being then curved so as to fit them." INGE, Society in Rome under the Caesars, p. 198.

9—K
"When Christianity appeared in the world, even the faint and imperfect impressions (concerning Polytheism) had lost much of their original power. Human reasons, which by its unassisted strength is incapable of perceiving the mysteries of faith, had already obtained an easy triumph over the folly of Paganism; and when Tertullian or Lactantius employ their labors in exposing its falsehood and extravagance, they are obliged to transcribe the eloquence of Cicero or the wit of Lucian. The contagion of these skeptical writings had been diffused far beyond the number of their readers. The fashion of incredulity was communicated from the philosopher to the man of pleasure or business, from the noble to the plebian, and from the master to the menial slave who waited at his table, and who eagerly listened to the freedom of his conversation. On public occasions the philosophic part of mankind affected to treat with respect and decency the religious institutions of their country; but their secret contempt penetrated through the thin and awkward disguise; and even the people, when they discovered that their deities were rejected and derided by those whose rank or understanding they were accustomed to reverence, were filled with doubts and apprehensions concerning the truth of those doctrines to which they had yielded the most implicit belief." GIBBON, Chap. 15, after N 151.

"But, if in the present instance a faith no longer believed was maintained out of political convenience, they amply made up for this in other respects. Unbelief and superstition, different hues of the same historical phenomenon, went in the Roman world of that day hand in hand, and there was no lack of individuals who in themselves combined both—who denied the gods with Epicurus, and yet prayed and sacrificed before every shrine." MOMMSEN, Book 5, Chap. 12,

9—L
"While Uzziah was in this state, and making preparations for futurity, he was corrupted in his mind by pride, and became inso-

lent, and this on account of that abundance which he had of things that will soon perish, and despised that power which is of eternal duration (which consisted in piety towards God, and in the observation of his laws); accordingly, when a remarkable day was come, and a general festival was to be celebrated, he put on the holy garment, and went into the temple to offer incense to God upon the golden altar, which he was prohibited to do by Azariah the high priest. In the meantime, a great earthquake shook the ground, and a rent was made in the temple, and the bright rays of the sun shone through it, and fell upon the king's face, insomuch that the leprosy seized upon him immediately; and before the city, at a place called Erpge, half the mountain broke off from the rest of the west, and rolled itself four furlongs, and stood still at the east mountain, till the roads, as well as the king's gardens, were spoiled by the obstruction." JOSEPHUS, Ant. 9-10-4.

9—M
"And the book of Daniel was showed him (Alexander), wherein Daniel declared that one of the Greeks should destroy the empire of the Persians, he supposed that himself was the person intended; and as he was then glad, he dismissed the multitude for the present, but the next day he called them to him, whereupon the; high priest desired that they might enjoy the laws of their forefathers, and might pay no tribute on the seventh year. He granted all they desire; and when they entreated him that he would permit the Jews in Babylon and Media to enjoy their own laws also, he willingly promised to do hereafter what they desired." JOSEPHUS, Ant. 11-8-5.

9—N
"And when the king (Epiphanes) had built an idol altar upon God's altar, he slew swine upon it, and so offered a sacrifice neither according to the law, nor the Jewish religious worship in that country. He also compelled them to forsake the worship which they paid their own God, and to adore those whom he took to be

gods; and made them build temples, and raise idol altars in every city and village, and offer swine upon them every day. He also commanded them not to circumcise their sons, and threatened to punish any that should be found to have transgressed his injunction. He also appointed overseers, who should compel them to do what he commanded. And indeed many Jews there were who complied with the king's commands, either voluntarily, or out of fear of the penalty that was denounced; but the best men, and those of the noblest souls, did not regard him, but did pay a greater respect to the customs of their country than concern as to the punishment which he threatened to the disobedient; on which account they every day underwent great miseries and bitter torments; for they were whipped with rods and their bodies were torn to pieces, and they were crucified while they were still alive and breathed; they also strangled those women and their sons whom they had circumcised, as the king had appointed, hanging their sons about their necks as they were upon the crosses. And if there were any sacred book of the law found, it was destroyed; and those with whom they were found, miserably perished also." JOSEPHUS, 12-5-4.

9—O
"This desolation (by Epiphanes) happened to the temple in the 145th year, on the 25th day of the month Appelleus, and on the 153rd olympaid; but it was dedicated anew, on the same day, the 25th of the month Appelleus, in the 148th year, and on the 154th olympaid. And this desolation came to pass according to the prophecy of Daniel, which was given 408 years before."—JOSEPHUS, Ant. 12-7-6.

9—P
"Hyrcanus took also Dora and Marissa, cities of Idumea, and subdued all the Idumeans; and permitted them to stay in that country, if they would circumcise their genitals, and make use of the laws of the Jews; and they were so desirous of living in the country of their forefathers, that they submitted to the use of cir-

cumcision, and the rest of the Jewish ways of living; at which time therefore this befell them, that they were hereafter no other than Jews." JOSEPHUS, Ant. 13-9-1.

9—Q
"And thus did this man (Herod) receive the kingdom having obtained it on the 184th olympaid, when Caius Domithis Calvinus was consul the second time, and Caius Asinius Pollio the first time." JOSEPHUS, Ant. 14-14-5, "And thus did the government of the Asamoneans cease, 126 years after it was first set up." JOSEPHUS, Ant. 14-16-4.

9—R
"Now Cyrenius, a Roman senator, and one who had gone through other magistracies, and had passed through them till he had been consul, and one who, on other accounts, was of great dignity, came at this time (after banishment of Archelaus, son of Herod the Great) into Syria, with a few others, being sent by Caesar to be a judge of that nation, and to take an account of their substance; Coponius also, a man of the equestrian order, was sent together with him, to have the supreme power over the Jews. Moreover, Cyrenius came himself into Judea, which was now added to the province of Syria, to take an account of their substance, and to dispose of Archelaus' money; but the Jews, although at the beginning they took the report of a taxation heniously, yet did they leave off any farther opposition to it, by the persuasion of Joazar, who was the son of Boethus, and high priest. So they, being over-persuaded, by Joazar's words, gave an account of their estates, without any dispute about it." JOSEPHUS, Ant. 18-1-1.

9—S
"Religion and morality were still compelling forces and ideas in the 1830's, and democracy, however disconnected with religion in the mind of the individual man, had sprung straight from the great religious movement of the Reformation. The claimed

Protestant right of each man to interpret the Bible for himself, to judge of creeds and ceremonies, to erect his own church and elect his own pastor, had been the solvent which had destroyed thrones and the old belief in divine right. The Protestant leaders had not believed in democracy, but their doctrines had led to it with complete inevitability." James Truslow Adams, Historian and critic in Atlantic Monthly, January, 1932, page 2.

9—T
"The early nineteenth century was still deeply religious, and the environment in which democratic ideas were coming in fruition was largely unaltered from that which had given them birth. Science was beginning to open limitless vistas of possible improvement to man without yet having reached the point of disillusioning him of his religious beliefs. It was a period, for enthusiastic souls, of apparently boundless possibilities in the future emphasized in the American case by our vast westward expansion. Uncritical optimism was rampant.

"Today all is changed. Science still promises possible extraordinary advances in the control of our physical environment, but for whole sections of the people it has destroyed old religious beliefs. Religion and morality as molding forces on our ideas have given place to science and efficiency." James Truslow Adams, historian and critic, in Atlantic Monthly, January, 1932, page 2.

9—U
"Choirs were formed as early as the fourth century; and the Council of Laodicea found it necessary to forbid congregational singing. But Gregory reformed the abuses, and restored music to the people. It is said that a copy of his Antiphonary is in possession of the monastery of St. Gall in Switzerland; a facsimile of which was published in 1867." SCHAFF-HERZOG ENCYCLOPAEDIA, Article—Music.

9—V

". . . Hence grave people objected to organ-playing as a frivolity, such as the Pagan Ammianus Marcellinus and the Christian Sidonius Apollinaria. Others, however, thought otherwise. A Frankish monk from the Merovingian time reckons it one of the great joys of future life, that there shall be perpetual organ-playing; from which passage it may also be learnt, that, at that time the organ was already used to accompany the hymn-singing of the service. It can consequently not have been something entirely new and altogether startling, when, in 757, King Pepin, received an organ as a present from the Byzantine emperor, Constantine Copronymus, or when Charlemagne ordered the organ presented to him by Michael Rhan have placed in the cathedral of Aix-le-Chapelle. . . In the Greek Church the organ never came into use. But after the eighth century it became more and more common in the Latin Church; not, however, without opposition from the side of the monks. Its misuse, however, raised so great an opposition to it, that, but for the Emperor Ferdinand, it would probably have been abolished by the Council of Trent." SCHAFF-HERZOG ENCYCLOPAEDIA. Article—Organ.

9—W

"In accordance with apostolic precept, the disciples spake to each other in psalms and hymns and spiritual songs. A body of devout lyrical poetry began to be formed—the work of Clement, Gregory Nazianzen, Ambrose, Hilary, and others—which during the middle and Reformation ages, was swelled to an immense volume by the contributions of many Christian poets. The church-singing was at first only a sort of monotonous (hypophonia) cantillation, in which all took part. This was improved into elaborate choral singing, which, like that of Milan, became, in the judgment of Augustine at least, too artificial and dramatic. The effect of this change was to exclude the people from taking part in the service. Congregational singing perished. Church music in all Roman and in many Protestant churches exhibits the furthest possible depar-

ture from the apostolic and primitive conception of that office."
SCHAFF-HERZOG ENCYCLOPAEDIA, Article—Worship.

9—X
"GREEK CHURCH, The, or more properly the Eastern Church, is both the source and background of the Western. Christianity arose in the East, and Greek was the language of the Scriptures and early services of the church, but when Latin Christianity established itself in Europe and Africa, and when the old Roman empire fell in two, and the eastern half became separate in government, interests, and ideas from the western, the term Greek or Eastern Church acquired gradually a fixed meaning. It denoted the church which included the patriarchates of Antioch, Alexandria, Jerusalem, and Constantinople, and their dependencies. The ecclesiastical division of the early church, at least within the empire, was based upon the civil. Constantine introduced a new partition of the empire into dioceses, and the church adopted a similar division. . . When the empire was divided, there was one patriarch in the West, the bishop of Rome, while in the East there were at first two, then four, and latterly five. This geographical fact has had a great deal to do in determining the character of the Eastern Church. It is not a despotic monarchy governed from one center and by a monarch in whom plentitude of power resides. It is an oligarchy of patriarchs. It is based, of course, on the great body of bishops; but episcopal rule, through the various grades of metropolitan, primate, exarch, attains to sovereignty only in the five patriarchal thrones. Each patriarch is, within his diocese, what the Galilean theory makes the pope in the universal church. He is supreme, and not amenable to any of his brother patriarchs, but is within the jurisdiction of an ecumenical synod. This makes the Greek Church quite distinct in government and traditions of polity from the Western.

"Conflict with Rome—The relation of the Greek Church to the Roman may be described as one of growing estrangement from the 5th to the 11th century, and a series of abortive attempts at reconciliation since the later date. The estrangement and final rupture may be traced to the overweening pretensions of the Roman bishops and to Western innovation in the doctrine of the Holy Spirit, accompanied by an alteration of creed. In the early church three bishops stood forth prominently, principally from the political eminence of the cities in which they ruled—the bishops of Rome, Alexandria, and Antioch. The transfer of the seat of empire from Rome to Constantinople gave the bishops of Rome a possible rival in the patriarch of Constantinople, but the absence of an overawing court and meddling statesmen did more than recoup the loss to the head of the Roman Church. . . . Political jealousies and interests intensified the disputes, and at last, after premonitory symptoms, the final break came in 1054, when Leo IX smote Michael Cerularius and the whole of the Eastern Church with an excommunication. Encyclopedia Britannica, Vol. XI. Article—Greek Church.

"HISTORICAL SURVEY—The Greek Church has no continuous history, like the Latin or the Protestant. She has long periods of monotony and stagnation; she is isolated from the main current of progressive Christendom; her languages and literature are little known among Western scholars. Yet this Church is the oldest in Christendom, and for several centuries she was the chief bearer of our religion. She still occupies the sacred territory of primitive Christianity, and claims most of the apostolic sees, as Jerusalem, Antioch, and the churches founded by Paul and John in Asia Minor and Greece. All the apostles, with the exception of Peter and Paul, labored and died in the East. From the old Greeks she inherited the language and certain national traits of character, while she incorporated into herself also much of Jewish and Oriental piety. She produced the first Christian Utenaiture, apologies of the Christian faith, refutations of heretics, commentaries of the Bible, sermons, homilies, and ascetic treaties." SCHAFF-HERZOG ENCYCLOPAEDIA, Vol. II. Article—Greek Church.

9—Y
"The Iconoclastic Controversy; the Popes become Temporal Sovereigns.—A dispute about the use of images in worship, known in church history as the 'War of the Iconoclasts,' which broke out in the eighth century between the Greek churches of the East and the Latin churches of the West, drew after it far-reaching consequences as respects the growing power of the Roman pontiff. Even long before the seventh century the churches both in the East and in the West had become crowded with images or pictures of the apostles, saints, and martyrs, which to the ignorant classes at least were objects of superstitious veneration. But the great disaster which just at this period befell the Church in the East—the irruption and conquests of the Arab Mohammedans—contributed to create among the Christians there a strong sentiment against the use of images as aids in worship. A party arose, who, like the party of reform among the ancient Hebrews, declared that God had given the Church over into the hands of the infidels because the Christians had departed from his true worship and fallen into idolatry. These opposers of the use of images in worship were given the name of Iconoclasts (image breakers). Leo the Isaurian, who came to the throne of Constantinople in 717, was a most zealous Iconoclast. The Greek churches of the East having been cleared of images, the Emperor resolved to clear also the Latin churches of the West of these symbols. To this end he issued a decree that they should not be used.

The bishop of Rome not only opposed the execution of the edict but by the ban of excommunication cut off the Emperor and all the iconoclastic churches of the East from communion with the true Catholic Church. Though images—paintings and mosaics only—were permanently restored in the Eastern churches in 842, still by this time other causes of alienation had arisen, and the breach between the two sections of Christendom could not now be closed. The final outcome was the permanent separation, in the last half of the eleventh century, of the Church of the East from that of the West. The former became known as the Greek,

Byzantine, or Eastern Church; the latter, as the Latin, Roman, or Catholic Church." MEDIAEVAL AND MODERN HISTORY by MYERS, Pages 31 and 32.

9—Z
"In the long period of twelve hundred years, which elapsed between the reign of Constantine and the reformation of Luther, the worship of saints and relics corrupted the pure and perfect simplicity of the Christian model; and some symptoms of degeneracy may be observed even in the first generations which adopted and cherished this pernicious innovation." GIBBON, Decline and Fall, Vol. 2, Chap. 28, page 615.

10—A
"C. Era, the era in use in all Christian countries, which was intended to commence with the birth of Christ. The era as now established was first used by Dionysius Exigiius (d. 545), who placed the birth of Christ on the 25th of December in the year of Rome 754, which year he counted as 1 A. D. This date for Christ's birth is now generally thought to be about four years too late." WEBSTER'S NEW INTERNATIONAL DICTIONARY; subhead under CHRISTIAN.

"From Josephus (Ant. 17-8-1; Wars, 1-33-8) we learn that Herod died in the thirty-seventh year of his reign. Now Herod was made king in the consulship of Cn. Domitius Calvinus and C. Asinius Pollio, i. e. B. C. 40 (714 A. U. IO.). Most writers have supposed that the year is reckoned by Josephus from the month Nisam; moreover, we may conclude from Josephus (Ant, 17-9-3) that Herod died at the beginning of the thirty-seventh year, or immediately before Passover. Consequently, we must add thirty-six years to 714 A. IL C. Henee we get 750 A. U. C., or B. C. 4 as the date of Herod's death, and since this took place subsequent to the birth of Jesus, B. C. 4 is the latest possible date that can be assigned to the birth of our Lord. (See Wieseler's Chronological Synopsis of the Four Gospels, Sec. 1, Chap. 2). Thus, our Christian era is really calculated from a wrong starting point. This was derived from the defective chronology of Dionysius Exiguus (6th century) who made the year of our Lord's nativity, or A. D. 1, correspond to 754 A. U. C." Owen C. Whitehouse in Bible Helps in International Series of Bible, under Chronology.

10—B
"A being of the nature of man, endowed with the same faculties, but with a longer measure of existence, would cast down a smile of pity and contempt on the crimes and follies of human ambition, so eager, in a narrow span, to grasp at a precarious and short-lived enjoyment. It is thus that the experience of history exalts and enlarges the horizon of our intellectual view. In a composition of some days, in a perusal of some hours, six hundred years have rolled away, and the duration of a life or reign is contracted to a fleeting moment; the grave is ever beside the throne; the success of a criminal is almost instantly followed by the loss of his prize; and our immortal reason survives and disdains the sixty phantoms of kings who have passed before our eyes, and faintly dwell on our remembrance. The observation that, in every age and climate, ambition has prevailed with the same commanding energy, may abate the surprise of a philosopher; but while he condemns the vanity, he may search the motive, of this universal desire to obtain and hold the sceptre of dominion." GIBBON, Chap. 48.

10—C
The government of the Church in first centuries can be indicated by the following brief taken from Mosheim: The terms Presbyters and Bishops referred to same order of men. 1-2-2-8

Presbyters were of equal importance in the infancy of the Church. 1-2-2-11

A bishop had authority over one congregation. 1-2-2-12

Power of bishops was extended by the following means: Bishops in cities had started churches in surrounding towns and villages, and in the 2nd century these were formed into provinces or dioceses over which the city bishop presided. 1-2-2-12 and 2-2-2-2

Congregations were independent through the 1st and part of the 2nd centuries. 1-2-2-14 and 2-2-2-2

Authority of the bishop extended in the administration of baptism. 1-2-4-8

In the 2nd century one bishop presided over each assembly with whom a council of presbyters was formed. To these presbyters the bishop distributed tasks. 2-2-2-1

Through part of the 2nd century the churches were still independent. But later in the century the churches of a province formed into one large ecclesiastical body which assembled at certain times, in order to deliberate about the common interests of the whole. Deputies of the several churches represented their respective churches in these meetings. These meetings were called councils. These councils did not exist before middle of 2nd century. 2-2-2-2, 3

These councils increased authority of the deputies or bishops by abolishing the rights of the people. Furthermore, the equality that had previously subsisted between all the bishops was set aside by the demand that some one of the provincial bishops should be invested with superior power and authority. This was the origin of the rights of Metropolitans. 2-2-2-3

The universal church brought by the councils to resemble a combination of a great number of little states. This brought into existence another order of ecclesiastics in different parts of the world who constituted the office of patriarchs. 2-2-2-3

In the 3rd century, one bishop in the larger cities was at the head of each church, acting in concert with the body of presbyters. Also, in the provinces one bishop had superiority over the other bishops. This condition helped pave the way for the general councils. 3-2-2-1

In the concentration of power, the bishops of Rome, Antioch and Alexandria acquired pre-eminence over all the rest. 3-2-2-1

The bishop of Rome was especially considered pre-eminent at this time. 3-2-2-2

Church government in the 3rd century degenerated by imperceptible steps, toward religious monarchy. The bishops, aspired to higher power, and encroached upon the rights of the people and also of the Presbyters. 3-2-2-3

The bishops appropriated the ensigns of temporal power and majesty, and were imitated by the presbyters. 3-2-2-4

Though Constantine "permitted" the church to remain distinct from the state, yet he assumed supreme power over it, and that by consent of the bishops. 4-2-2-1

Lesser councils were convened which were presided over by provincial bishops, in which were deliberated matters pertaining to the churches of the province. 4-2-2-1

To the provincial councils were added the general ecumenical councils, composed of delegates from all the world. These councils were established by authority of the emperor. 4-2-2-1

The power of the bishops was increased after the reign of Constantine, for they excluded the people, and finally the presbyters, from all ecclesiastical affairs. 4-2-2-2

Only a shadow of ancient government of the Church left at close of 4th century. 4-2-2-2

The rights of the universal church were transferred to the emperors. 4-2-2-2

In suiting the administration of the Church to changes in civil government, new degrees of rank were introduced among the bishops. The bishops of Rome, Antioch, Alexandria, and Constantinople were given more preeminence, and the title of Patriarchs was given them. Next in order came the Exarchs who had inspection over several provinces. Next archbishops over districts. Next bishops with variable authority. Next chorepiscopi or superintendents over country churches. 4-2-2-3

Constantine provided for the distinction of the external government of the Church for the civil authority, and the internal for the bishops. This order was interchanged. 4-2-2-4

On account of a great variety of causes, the bishop of Rome was first in rank and was distinguished by a sort of pre-eminence over all other prelates. Some of the reasons for the pre-eminence of the bishop of Rome were: the magnificence and splendor of the church over which he presided; riches of his revenues and possessions; the number and variety of his ministers; his credit with the people; and his splendid manner of living. 4-2-S-5

The ecclesiastical laws in the 4th century were enacted either by the emperor or by the councils. 4-2-2-6

Steps were laid in the 4th century by which the bishops of Rome afterwards reached supreme power. 4-2-2-6

In 4th century one Acrius denied any divine distinction between bishops and presbyters. He also made other demands for return to primitive simplicity. 4-2-3-21

Power of the bishops was influenced by the political state of the Empire. 5-2-2-1

Five patriarchs created with superior power. 5-2-2-2, 3

Contention for power between patriarchs, bishops and the lower orders. 5-2-2-4

Several circumstances imperceptibly were establishing universal supremacy of the bishop of Rome in the 5th century, although he had not yet assumed such authority. 5-2-2-6

No remarkable change in church government in 6th century. 6-2-2-1

Bishops of Rome and Constantinople vie with each other for authority. 6-2-2-1

The Roman pontiff aims at unlimited power. 6-2-2-2

Papal supremacy first introduced. 7-2-2-1

Many private persons opposed the vices and ambitions of the Roman pontiffs, and retired to the valleys in order to obtain liberty. 7-2-2-S

10—D
"II. (Character of MOHAMMED—It is written in the Koran. If restored to chronological order, it shows a gradual change of tone. In the earliest Suras, the wild rhapsodic poetry prevails; in the next, the missionary and narrative element; in the letter, he commands as legislator warrior. This suggests a change in the character of this remarkable man, who ranks with Confucius and Sakya Muni as a lawgiver of nations. He began as a poor and ignorant camel-driver, and ended as the poet, prophet, and king of Arabia, and the founder of a religion which at one time threat-

ened to conquer the civilized world. He was for a long time abhorred in the Christian Church as a wicked imposter, as the Antichrist, as the false prophet of the Apocalypse, as the first-born of Satan. But the modern historians give him credit for sincerity in his first period. . . Mohammed consolidated and energized this reform-movement. At first he suffered much persecution, which would have discouraged any ordinary man. In his Mecha period he revealed no impure and selfish motives. He used only moral means; he preached, and warned the people against the sin of idolatry. He was faithful to his one wife. But his great success in Medina spoiled him. He degenerated, like Solomon. He became the slave of ambition and sensual passion. He first preached tolerance, but afterwards used the sword for the propagation of his religion. He watched in cold blood the massacre of six hundred Jews in one day, and commanded the extermination of all idolators in Arabia, unless they submitted in four months. After the death of Chadijah, he married gradually fourteen or fifteen wives, and left at his death nine widows, besides slave-concubines. He claimed special revelations for exceptional liberty of sexual indulgence and the marriage of relatives forbidden to ordinary Moslems. In his fifty-third year he married Ayesha, a girl of nine. He maintained, however, the simplicity of a Bedouin sheik to the end. He lived with his wives in lowly cottages, was temperate in meat and drink, milked his goats, mended his sandals and clothes, and aided his wives in cooking and sewing. He was of medium size, broad-shouldered, with black eyes and hair, a long nose, a patriarchal beard, and a commanding look. He had no learning, but fervid imagination, poetic genius, and religious enthusiasm. He was liable to fantastic hallucinations and altercations of high excitement and deep depression. His nervous temperament and epilepsy help to explain his revelations, whether pretended or real." PHILIP SCHAFF in SCHAFF-HERZOG Encyclopedia.

"In his private conduct, Mohamet indulged the appetites of a man, and abused the claims of a prophet. A special revelation dispensed him from the law's which he had imposed on his nation; the female sex, without reserve, was abandoned to his desires; and this singular prerogative excited the envy, rather than the scandal, the veneration, rather than the envy, of the devout Mussulmans. If we remember the seven hundred wives and three hundred concubines of the wise Solomon, we shall applaud the modesty of the Arabian, who espoused no more than seventeen or fifteen wives; eleven are enumerated who occupied at Medina their separate apartments round the house of the apostle, and enjoyed in their turns the favor of his conjugal society. What is singular enough, they were all widows, excepting only Ayesha, the daughter of Abubeker, She was doubtless a virgin, since Mahomet consummated his nuptials (such is the premature ripeness of the climate) when she was only nine years of age. The youth, the beauty, the spirit of Ayesha, gave her a superior ascendant; she was beloved and trusted by the prophet; and, after his death, the daughter of Abubeker was long revered as the mother of the faithful. Her behavior had been ambiguous and indiscreet; in a nocturnal march she was accidentally left behind; and in the morning Ayesha returned to the camp with a man. The temper of Mahomet was inclined to jealousy; but a divine revelation assured him of her innocence; he chastised her accusers, and published a law of domestic peace, that no woman should be condemned unless four male witnesses has seen her in the act of adultery. In his adventures with Zeineb, the wife of Zeid, and with Mary, an Egyptian captive, the amorous prophet forgot, the interest of his reputation. At the house of Zeid, his freedman and adopted son, he beheld, in a loose undress, the beauty of Zeineb, and burst forth into an ejaculation of devotion and desire. The servile, or grateful, freedman understood the hint, and yielded without hesitation to the love of his benefactor. But as the filial relation had excited some doubt and scandal, the angel Gabriel descended from heaven to ratify the deed, to annul the adoption, and gently to reprove the apostle for distrusting the indulgence of his God. One of his wives, Hafna, the daughter of Omar, surprised him on her own bed, in the embraces of his Egyptian captive; she promised secrecy and forgiveness; he swore that he would renounce the possession of Mary. Both parties forgot their engagements; and Gabriel again descended with a chapter of the Koran, to absolve him from his oath, and to exhort him freely to enjoy his captives and concubines, without listening to the clamors of his wives. In a solitary retreat of thirty days, he labored, alone with Mary, to fulfill the commands of the angel. When his love and revenge were satiated, he summoned to his presence his eleven wives, reproached their disobedience and indiscretion, and threatened them with a sentence of divorce, both in this world and in the next; a dreadful sentence, since those who had ascended the bed of the prophet were forever excluded from the hope of a second marriage." GIBBON, Decline and Fall. Chap. 50.

10—E

"III. THE MOHAMMEDAN RELIGION, so called after its founder, or ISLAM, so called after its chief duty and virtue (resignation to Allah), is one of the three monotheistic creeds which sprung from the Semitic race. It is an eclectic system, composed of Jewish, heathen, and Christian elements, which were scattered through Arabia before Mohammed. It borrowed monotheism and many rites and ceremonies from the Jews, and may be called a bastard Judaism, descended from Ishmael and Esau. It was professedly a restoration of the faith of Abraham. In relation to Christianity, it may be called the great Unitarian heresy of the East. Christ is acknowledged as the greatest prophet next to Mohammed, conceived by the Virgin Mary, at the appearance of Gabriel, under a palm tree, but only a man. God has no wife, and therefore no son. . . . Jesus predicted the coming of Mohammed, when he promised the Paraclete. He will return to judgment. The Christian elements in the Koran are borrowed from apocryphal and heretical sources, not from the canonical Gospels. With these corrupt Jewish and Christian traditions are mixed, in a moderated form, the heathen elements of sensuality, polygamy, slavery, and the use of violence in the spread of religion. . . . The fundamental article of Islam is, 'There is no God but Allah, and Mohammed is his prophet.' It has six articles of faith—God, predestination (fatalism), the angels (good and bad), the books (chiefly the Koran), the prophets, the resurrection and judgment, with eternal reward and punishment. . . . Slavery, polygamy, and concubinage are allowed. Ordinary Moslems are restricted to four wives; pachas, caliphs, and sultans may fill their harems to the extent of their wishes and means. Woman, in Mohammedan countries, is always veiled, and mostly ignorant and slavishly dependent. In nothing is the superiority of Christianity more striking than in the superior condition of woman and home life. Believers are promised a sensual paradise, with blooming gardens, fresh fountains, and an abundance of beautiful virgins. Infidels, and those who refuse to fight for their faith, will be cast into one of the seven hells beneath the lowest earth and seas of darkness." PHILIP SCHAFF in SCHAFF-HERZOG Encyclopedia.

"It is natural enough that an Arabian prophet should dwell with rapture on the groves, the fountains, and the rivers of Paradise; but instead of inspiring the blessed inhabitants with a liberal taste for harmony and science, conversation and friendship, he idly celebrates the pearls and diamonds, the robes of silk, palaces of marble, dishes of gold, rich wines, artificial dainties, numerous attendants, and the whole train of sensual and costly luxury, which becomes insipid to the owner, even in the short period of his mortal life. Seventy-two Houris, or black-eyed girls, of respondent beauty, blooming youth, virgin purity, and exquisite sensibility, will be created for the use of the meanest believer; a moment of pleasure will be prolonged to a thousand years, and his faculties will be increased a hundred-fold, to render him worthy of his felicity. Notwithstanding a vulgar prejudice, gates of heaven will be open to both sexes; but Mahomet has not specified the male companions of the female elect, lest he should alarm the jealousy of their former husbands, or disturb their felicity, by the suspicion of an everlasting marriage." GIBBON, Chapter 50.

10—F
"CHRISTMAS, a Christian festival celebrated on Dec. 25, in memory of the birth of Jesus Christ. The English name Christmas, like the Dutch Kerstmisse, or Kersmis, is formed analogous to such names as Candlemas, Michaelmas, etc. In the Romanic languages the name is derived from the Latin Natalis, Natalitia or Nativitas; Italian Natal, Spanish Nadal, or Natividad, French Noel. The German Weibnacht is a literal translation of the Hebrew Chanuka, the name of the Jewish festival of the dedication of purification of the temple by Judas Maccabaeus. The Scandinavian Jaul, and the Anglo-Saxon Geol, mean 'wheel,' and refer to the winter solstice.

When the festival of Christmas is first spoken of in the ancient Church (CLEMENT OF ALEXANDRIA: Stromata, lip. 1., cap. 21), it was celebrated by the Eastern Church on Jan. 6, under the name of Epiphania, and by the Western Church on Dec. 25, under the name of Natali. This discrepancy is easily accounted for, however, by the circumstance that the gospel gives no date of Christ's birth, but simply tells that it took place during night. . . . What foundation there originally was for the Roman date of Dec. 25 is difficult to decide. On account of this date, some connect the Christian festival of Christmas with the above-mentioned Jewish feast, Chanuka; and many features seem to speak for such a relation between them. Others connect with the Saturnalia, or Brumalia, or some other Pagan Roman feast; and here, too, the single features are often strikingly resemblant. . . . The date once fixed, Christmas gradually became one of the three great annual festivals of the Church. The whole period from Nativity to Epiphany was consecrated,—Dec. 26 as memorial of the martyr Stephen; Dec. 27, of St. John; Dec. 28, of the Massacre of the Innocents, etc. The four Sundays preceding Christmas were incorporated with the cycle, under the title of Advent, as a preparation for the festival. The day itself was celebrated by three masses—one in the night, one at daybreak, and one in the morning; and the costliest utensils and furniture were used. During the middle ages the celebration assumed, in accordance with the taste of the time, quite a theatrical aspect. The manger was shown, with the Virgin sitting beside it, surrounded with chanting angels. The wise men, the shepherds, Joseph, etc., were also represented; and a complete Mystery was formed. As a remnant of this symbolical representation of biblical events which formerly found so much favor both with the priests and with their flocks, it may be mentioned, that, in the third decade of the present century, the custom was still kept of rocking a doll, in a cradle adorned with lights, on the top of the spire of the Cathedral of Tubingen at twelve o'clock Christmas night, while a band of wind instruments blew the Hymn of the Nativity.

No other Christian festival penetrated so deeply into the household as Christmas, probably because its character is essentially joy. Such as it appears in the household, however, many features indicate that there were non-Christian elements present in its origin. The use of lighted tapers reminds forcibly of the Jewish festival of purification. The giving of presents was a Roman custom. The Yule tree and the Yule-log are remnants of old Teutonic nature-worship. In the household, also, the festival gradually sank down into a mere revelry." SCHAFF-HERZOG ENCYCLOPAEDIA.

"The eastern Christians celebrated the memory of Christ's birth and baptism in one festival, which was fixed on the sixth of January, and this day was by them called Epiphany, as on it the immortal Saviour was manifested to the world. On the other hand, the Christians of the west seem to have always celebrated the birth of our Lord on the 25th of December; for there appears to be very little certainty in the accounts of those, who allege, that the Roman pontiff, Julius 1 removed the festival of Christ's birth from the 6th of January to the 25th of December." MOSHEIM, 4-24-5.

"CHRISTMAS DAY, (French, Noel from Dies Natalis; German, Weihanehtsfest; Old Eng. and Seand., Yule; Ang.-Sax., Geol), a festival of the Christian church, observed on the 25th of December, in memory of the birth of Jesus Christ. There is, however, a difficulty in accepting this as the date of the Nativity, December being the height of the rainy season in Judea, when neither flocks nor shepherds could have been at night in the fields of Bethlehem.

"By the 5th century, however, whether from the influence of some tradition, or from the desire to supplant heathen festivals of that period of the year, such as the Saturnalia, the 25th of December had been generally agreed upon. Augustine expressly mentioned this date (DeTrin. IV. 5); and Chrysostom seems to speak of it as a custom imported from the West within ten years. Before that time, it appears to have been kept conjointly with the feast of the Epiphany on the 6th of January. It is generally considered to rank third among the festivals of the church (Easter and Whitsuntide alone being placed above it) and to have a joy peculiarly its own." ENCYCLOPAEDIA BRITANNICA.

10—G

"Easter, the festival of our Lord's resurrection and with Christmas the most joyous day observed by the Church. Term—The term is derived from the Saxon Ostara, or Eostre (German Ostern), the goddess of Spring. The French designation paques preserves a reference to the Jewish pascha, or passover. In the early church pascha designated the festival of Christ's crucifixion. After the second century (Neander, Hilgenfiold, etc.) or according to others, after the third or fourth (Steitz), it designated both the festival of the crucifixion and the resurrection. Subsequently the term was limited to the latter. Only a single instance is the original rendered Easter (Acts 12:4) in our version; in all other cases, passover. The Revised Version has rectified this inconsistency in translation.

Date.—In the early church there was no uniformity in the day observed (Epiphan., Hoer., LXX.). Bede at a later date makes frequent reference to this discrepancy, and mentions, that, while Queen Eanfelda was keeping Palm Sunday, King Oswy was observing Easter (about 651). The present (Or Nicene) rule seems to have been adopted in England by Archbishop Theodore, in 669. A party called the Quartodecimani, or Fourteeners (Greek TETRADITAI and TETRADEKA-TITAI) observed the day (of crucifixion) on the 14th of Nisah, no matter on what day of the week it fell. The Western Church deviated from this custom; und Polycarp, on a visit to Rome (154), endeavored in vain to persuade Aniectus to adopt the quartodeeiman mode. Victor of Rome (197) was only restrained by public opinion, and the protests of Irenaeus, from excommunicating the Quartodecimans, to grave an offence was it considered to observe the 14th. The Council of Nicaea (325) decreed that there should be uniformity in the date of observance. It is not in place here to go further into the question of the ancient controversy on the date of Easter. See Article—PASCHAL CONTROVERSIES. It is, however, proper to state the results of the decree of Nicaea which determines our date of Easter. By that decree it is fixed on the Sunday immediately following the fourteenth day of the so-called Paschal moon, which happens on or first after the vernal equinox. The vernal equinox invariably falls on March 21. Easter, then, cannot occur earlier than March 22, or later than April 25." SCHAFF-HERZOG ENCYCLOPAEDIA.

"The Christians of this (2d) century celebrated anniversary festivals in commemoration of the death and resurrection of Christ, and of the effusion of the Holy Ghost upon the apostles. The day which was observed as the anniversary of Christ's death, was called the paschal day, or passover, because it was looked upon to be the same with that on which the Jews celebrated the feast of that name." MOSHEIM, 2-2-4-9.

"EASTER, the annual festival observed throughout Christendom in commemoration of the Resurrection of our Lord Jesus Christ. The word Easter—Anglo-Saxon, Eastre, Eoster; German, Ostera—like the names of the days of the week, is a survival from the old Teutonic mythology. According to Bede it is derived from Eostre, or Ostara, the Anglo-Saxon goddess of spring, to whom the fourth month answering to our April—thence called Eosturmonath—was dedicated. This month Bede informs us, was the same as the 'Mensis Paschalis,' when 'the old festival was observed with the gladness of a new solemnity.' . . . There is no trace of the celebration of Easter as a Christian festival in the New Testament or in the writings of the apostolic fathers." ENCYCLOPAEDIA BRITTANNICA, Article—EASTER.

10—H
"During almost a year which Alexander continued in Babylon, he revolved a great many projects in his mind; such as to go round Africa by sea, to make a complete discovery of all the nations lying round the Caspian Sea, and inhabiting its coasts; to conquer Arabia, to make war with Carthage, and to subdue the rest of Europe. The very thoughts of sitting still fatigued him, and the great vivacity of his imagination and ambition would never suffer him to be at rest; nay, could he have conquered the whole world, he would have sought a new one, to satiate the avidity of his desires." ROLLIN'S ANCIENT HISTORY, Vol. 3, page 351.

"Alexander's desire was to extend his conquests to the Ganges, but his soldiers began to murmur because of the length and hardness of their campaigns, and he reluctantly gave up the undertaking. . . . In the midst of his vast projects Alexander was seized by a fever, brought on doubtless by his insane excesses, and died at Babylon, 323 B. C. in the thirty-second year of his age." MYERS ANCIENT HISTORY, pages 279, 282.

"The most remarkable part of Alexander's career now commences. An ordinary conqueror would have been satisfied with the submission of the great capitals, and would have awaited, in the luxurious abodes which they offered, the adhesion of the more distant provinces. But for Alexander rest possessed no attractions. So long as there were lands or men to conquer, it was his delight to subjugate them. The pursuit of Darius and then of Bessus, drew him on to the north-eastern corner of the Persian Empire, whence the way was open into a new world, generally believed to be one of immense wealth. From Bactria and Sogdiana, Alexander proceeded through Afghanistan to India, which he entered on the side whence alone India is accessible by land, viz., the northwest. At first, he warred with the princes who held their governments adepdtiennies of Persia; but, when these had submitted, he desired still to press eastward, and complete the subjugation of the continent, which was believed to terminate at no great distance. The refusal of his soldiers to proceed stopped him at the Sutlej, and forced him to relinquish his designs, and to bend his steps homeward.

"It was the intention of Alexander, after taking the measures which he thought advisable for the consolidation of his empire, and the improvement of his intended capital, Babylon, to attempt the conquest Of the peninsula of Arabia—a vast tract inconveniently interposed between his western and his eastern provinces. A fleet under Nearchus, was to have proceeded along the coast, while Alexander, with an immense host, traversed the interior. But these plans were brought to an end, by the sudden death of their projector at Babylon in the thirteenth year of his reign and the thirty-third of his age, June, B. C. 323. This premature demise makes it impossible to determine whether, or not, the political wisdom of Alexander was on a par with his strategic ability—whether, or no, he would have succeeded in consolidating and uniting his heterogeneous conquests, and have proved the Darius as well as the Cyrus of his empire. Cut off unexpectedly in the vigor of early manhood, he left no inheritor, either of his power or of his projects. The empire which he had constructed broke into fragments soon after his death; and his plans, whatever they were, perished with him." GEORGE RAWLINSON in "A Manual of Ancient History." pp. 235, 237.

10—I
"Trajan was ambitious of fame; and as long as mankind shall continue to bestow more liberal applause on their destroyers than on their benefactors, the thirst of military glory will ever be the vice of the most exalted characters. The praises of Alexander, transmitted by a succession of poets and historians, had kindled a dangerous emulation in the mind of Trajan. Like him, the Roman emperor undertook an expedition against the nations of the East; but he lamented with a sigh, that his advanced age scarcely left him any hopes of equaling the renown of the son of Philip. . . . In the purer ages of the commonwealth the use of arms was reserved for those ranks of citizens who had a country to love, a property to defend, and some share in enacting those laws, which it was their interest as well as duty to maintain. But in proportion as the public freedom was lost in extent of conquest, war was gradually improved into an art, and degraded, into a trade. The legions themselves, even at the time when they were recruited in the most distant provinces, were supposed to consist of Roman citizens. That distinction was generally considered, either as a legal qualification or as a proper recompense for the soldier; but a more serious regard was paid to the essential merit of age, strength, and military stature." GIBBON, Chapter I.

10—J
"For eight years all Asia was astir with the work of preparation. (for the expedition against Greece) Levies were made upon all the provinces that acknowledged the authority of the Great King, (Xerxes I) from India to Macedonia, from the regions of the Oxus to those of the Upper Nile. From all the maritime states upon the Mediterranean were demanded vast contingents of war galleys, transport ships, and naval stores. While these land and sea forces were being gathered and equipped, gigantic works were in progress on the Thracian coast and on the Hellespont to insure

the safety and facilitate the march of the coming hosts." MYERS Ancient History, page 191.

"Xerxes thus levied his army searching out every region of the continent. For from the reduction of Egypt, he was employed four whole years in assembling his forces, and providing things necessary for the expedition, (against Greece) In the course of the fifth year he began his march with a vast multitude of men. For of the expeditions with which we are acquainted, this was by far the greatest, so that that of Darius against the Scythians appears, nothing in comparison with this." Herodotus, Book 7, Sections 19, 20.

"Xerxes, in the four years which followed on the reduction of Egypt, continued incessantly to make the most gigantic preparations for his intended attack upon Greece, and among them included all the precautions which a wise foresight could devise in order to ward off every conceivable peril. A general order was issued to all satraps throughout the Empire, calling on them to levy the utmost force of their province for the new war; while, as the equipment of Oriental troops depends greatly on the purchase and distribution of arms by their commander, a rich reward was promised to the satrap whose contingent should appear at the appointed place and time in the most gallant array. . . His army is said to have accompanied him; but more probably it joined him in the spring, flocking in, contingent after contingent, from the various provinces of his vast Empire. Forty-nine nations, according to Herodotus, served under his standard." Rawlinson, Five Great Monarchies, Vol. 3, Chapter 7, pp. 448, 452.

"All these expeditions, and any others, if there have been any besides them, are not to be compared with this one. For what nation did not Xerxes lead out of Asia against Greece? What stream, being drunk, did not fail him, except that of great rivers. Some supplied ships; others were ordered to furnish men for the infantry, from others cavalry were required, from others transports for horses, together with men to serve in the army; others had to furnish long ships for the bridges, and others provisions and vessels." Herodotus, Book 7, See. 21.

10—K
"The Decline and Fall of the Persian Empire.—The power and supremacy of the Persian monarchy passed away with the reign of Xerxes. The last one hundred and forty years of the existence of the empire was a time of weakness and anarchy, and presents nothing that need claim our attention in this place.

"In the year 334 B. C., Alexander the Great, king of Macedonia, led a small army of Greeks and Macedonians across the Hellespont intent upon the conquest of Asia. His succeeding movements and the establishment of the short-lived Macedonian monarchy upon the ruins of the Persian Empire are matters that properly belong to Grecian history, and will be related at a later stage of our story." Myers Ancient History, page 94. (Note that Myers passes immediately from Xerxes to the time of Alexander. See Daniel 11:2, 3).

From Xerxes we have to date at once the decline of the Empire in respect to territorial greatness and military strength, and likewise its deterioration in regard to administrative vigor and national spirit." Rawlinson, Five Great Monarchies, Vol. 3, Chap. 7, Page 471.

10—L
"And when he shall stand up, his kingdom shall be broken," by his death, "and shall be divided towards the four winds of heaven and not to his posterity, nor according to his dominion which he ruled; for his kingdom shall be plucked up, even for others beside those namely, besides the four greater princes. We have already seen the vast empire of Alexander parceled out into four great kingdoms; without including those foreign princes who founded other kingdoms in Cappadocia, Armenia, Bithynia, Heraelea,

and on the Bosphorus, All this was present to Daniel." ROLLIN, "Vol. 3, Page 597.

"Consequently, the vast empire created by Alexander's unparalleled conquests was distracted by the wrangling and wars of his successors, and before the close of the fourth century B. C. had become broken into many fragments. Besides minor states, four monarchies rose out of the ruins." Myers Ancient History, Page 286.

10—M
"The commotions and revolts which happened in. the east, making Antiochus (Theos) weary of his war with King Ptolemy (Philadelphus), peace was made between them on the terms, that Antiochus, divorcing Laodice, his former wife, should marry Bernice, daughter of Ptolemy, and make her his queen instead of the other, and entail his crown upon the male issue of that marriage. And this agreement being ratified on both sides, for the full performance of it, Antiochus put away Laodice, though she were his sister by the same father, and he had two sons born to him by her; and Ptolemy carrying his daughter to Pelusium, there put her on board his fleet, and sailed with her to Selucia, a sea-port town near the mouth of the River Orontes in Syria; where having met Antiochus, he delivered his daughter to him, and the marriage was celebrated with great solemnity. And thus 'the king's daughter of the south came, and was married to the king of the north'; and, by virtue of that marriage, 'an agreement was made between those two kings,' according to the prophecy of the prophet Daniel, 11:5, 6. For in that place, by the king of the south, is meant the king of Egypt, and by the king of the north, the king of Syria; and both are there so-called in respect of Judea, which lying between these two countries, hath Egypt on the south, and Syria on the north. For the fuller understanding of this prophecy, it is to be observed, that the holy prophet, after having spoken of Alexander the Great (ver. 3) and of the four kings among whom his empire was divided (ver. 4) confines the rest of his prophecy

in that chapter to two of them only, that is to the king of Egypt, and the king of Syria, and first he begins with that king of Egypt who first reigned in that country after Alexander, that is, Ptolemy' Soter, whom he calls king of the south, and saith of him that he should be strong. And that he was so, all that write of him do sufficiently testify; for he had under him Egypt, Libya Cyrene, Arabia, Palestine, Coele-Syria, most of the maritime provinces of Lesser Asia, the island of Cyprus, several of the isles of the Aegean Sea, now called the Archipelago, and some cities also in Greece, as Sicyon, Corinth, and others. And then the prophet proceedeth to speak of the four successors (or princes, as he calls them) of Alexander, and he was Beleueus Nicator king of the north; of whom he saith, that he 'should be strong above the king of the south, and have great dominion also above him'; that is, greater than the king of the south. And that he had so, appears from the large territories he was possessed of; for he had under him all the countries of the east, from Mount Taurus to the River Indus, and several of the provinces of Lesser Asia, also from Mount Taurus to the Aegean Sea; and he had moreover added to them, before his death, Thrace and Macedon. And then, in the next place (ver. 6) he tells us of the coming of the king's daughter of the south, after the end of several years, to the king of the north, and the agreement, or treaty of peace, which should thereon be made between those two kings Which plainly points out unto us this marriage of Bernice, daughter of Ptolemy Philadelphus king of Egypt, with Antiochus Theus king of Syria, and the peace which was thereon made between them; for all this was exactly transacted according to what was predicted by the holy prophet in this prophecy. After this the holy prophet proceeds, through the rest of the chapter to foreshadow all the other most remarkable events that were brought to pass in the transactions of the succeeding times of those two races of kings, till the death of Antiochus Epiphanes, the great persecutor of the Jewish nation: all which I shall take notice of in the following series of this history, and apply them to the prophecy for the explication of it, as they come in my way." PRIDEAUX'S CONNEXION, year 249.

"Details of this Reign. (That of Antiochus Theos)—Marriage of Antiochus with Laodice, daughter of Achaeus. Her influence, and that of his sister Apame, wife of Matas, engaged him in war with Ptolemy Philadelphus, B. C. 260, which is terminated, B. C. 252, by a marriage between Antiochus and Berenice, Ptolemy's daughter. Soon after the close of this war, B. C. 255, Parthia and Bactria revolt and establish their independence. On the death of Philadelphus, B. C. 247, Antiochus repudiates Berenice and takes back his former wife Laodice, who however, doubtful of his constancy, murders him to secure the throne for her son, Seleucus, B. C. 246." RAWLINSON, Ancient History, page 251.

"As soon as Antiochus Theos had received intelligence of the death of Ptolemy Philadelphus, his father-in-law, he divorced Berenice, and recalled Laodice and her children. This lady, who knew the variable disposition and inconstancy of Antiochus, and was apprehensive that the same levity of mind would induce him to supplant her, by receiving Berenice again, resolved to improve the present opportunity to secure the crown for her son. Her own children were disinherited by the treaty made with Ptolemy; by which it was also stipulated that the issue Berenice might have by Antiochus should succeed to the throne, and she then had a son. Laodice, therefore, caused Antiochus to be poisoned. . . . Laodice, not believing herself safe as long as Berenice and her son lived, concerted measures with Seleucus to destroy them also; but that princess, being informed of their design, escaped the danger for some time by retiring, with her son, to Daphne, where she shut herself up in the asylum built by Seleucus Nicator; but being at last betrayed by the perfidy of those who besieged her there, by the order of Laodice, first her son, and then herself, with all the Egyptians who had accompanied her to that retreat were murdered in the basest and most inhuman manner." ROLLIN, Vol. 3, Book 16, Chap. 3, See, 1,

148 | *Historical Quotations*

10—N
"While Berenice (daughter of Philadelphus and former wife of Antiochus Theus) continued shut up and besieged in Daphne, the cities of Lesser Asia, hearing of her distress, commiserated her ease, and immediately, by a joint association, sent an army toward Antioch for her relief; and Ptolemy Euregetes, her brother, hastened thither with a greater force out of Egypt for the same purpose. But both Berenice and her son were cut off before either of them could arrive for their help; whereupon both armies turning their desire of saving the queen and her son into a rage for the revenging of their death, the Asian forces joined the Egyptians for the effecting of it, and Ptolemy, at the head of both, carried all before him; for he not only slew Laodice, but also made 'himself master of all Syria and Cilicia, and then passing the Euphrates, brought all under him as far as Babylon, and the River Tigris, and would have subjugated to him all the other provinces of the Syrian empire, but that a sedition arising in Egypt during his absence called him back to suppress it." PRIDEAUX'S CONNEXION, year 246. See also Rollin, Vol. 3, Chap. 3, See. 1. Rawlinson, Ancient History, page 272; Schaff-Herzog, Article—Ptolemy.

10—O
"Ptolemy III, Euergetes, ("well-doer"), B. C. 247-222; alluded to in Dan. 11:7-9; invaded Syria in 246, to avenge the repudiation and murder of his sister, Berenice (See Antiochus II, p. 95), and had conquered it as far north as Antioch, and was moving eastward towards Babylon, when he was recalled by troubles at home. His policy towards the Jews in Egypt was generous; while, in token of his victories, he sacrificed in the temple at Jerusalem 'after the custom of the law' (Joseph: C. Ap., 11:5). He brought back to Memphis the gods taken from Egypt by Cambyses. It was for this he received his epithet, 'well-doer.'" SCHAFF-HERZOG. Article—Ptolemy III.

"And therefore, having appointed Antiochus and Xantippus, two of his generals, the former of them to command the provinces he had taken on the west side of Mount Taurus, and the other to command the provinces he had taken on the east side of it, he marched back into Egypt, carrying with him vast treasures, which he had gotten together, in the plunder of the conquered provinces; for he brought from thence with him forty thousand talents of silver, a vast number of precious vessels of silver and gold, and images also to the number of two thousand five hundred, among which were many of the Egyptian idols, which Cambyses, on his conquering Egypt, had carried thence into Persia. These Ptolemy (son of Philadelphus and brother of Berenice) having restored to their former temples, on his return from this expedition, he thereby much endeared himself to his people." PRIDEAUX, year 246.

10—P
"The weakness of Philopator, and the mismanagement of the State by Sosiblus, who at once incapable and wicked, laid the empire open to attack; and it was not long before the young king of Syria, Antiochus III, took advantage of the condition of affairs to advance his own pretensions to the possessions of the long-disputed tract between Syria Proper and Egypt. . . . Details of the War. Antiochus commenced B. C. 219, by besieging Seleuceia, the port of Antioch, which had remained in the hands of the Egyptians since the great invasion, of Euergetes. Being joined by Theodotus, the Egyptian governor of Coele- Syria, he invaded that country, took Tyre and Ptolemais (Acre), and advanced to the frontiers Of Egypt." RAWLINSON, A. M., p. 275. See also Rollin, Vol. 4, pp. 142, 143. PRIDEAUX; year 221, etc.

10—Q
"Ptolemy, Philopator was an indolent, effiminate prince. It was necessary to excite and drag him, in a manner, out of his lethargy, in order to prevail with him to take up arms, and repulse the enemy, who were preparing to march into his country. At last, he put himself at the head of his troops; and, by the valor and good conduct of his generals, obtained a signal victory over Antiochus (the Great) at Raphia." ROLLIN, Vol. 4, Page 143.

"It might have been expected that, under the circumstances, he (Antiochus the Great) would have been successful. But the Egyptian forces, relaxed though their discipline had been by Sosibius, were still superior to the Syrians; and the battle of Raphia (B.C. 217) was a repetition of the lessons taught at Pelusium and Gaza. The invader was once more defeated upon the borders, and by the peace which followed, the losses of the two preceding years were, with one exception, recovered (by Philopator). . . In the third year of the war, B. C. 217, Philopator marched out from Alexandria in person, with 70,000 foot, 5,000 horse and 73 elephants. Antiochus advanced to give him battle, and the two armies met at Rephia, on the eastern edge of the desert. After a vain attempt on the part of Theodotus to assassinate Philopator in his camp, an engagement took place, and Antiochus was completely defeated. He then made peace, relinquishing all his conquests but Seleuceia." RAWLINSON, A. H., page 275. See also SCHAFF-HERZOG, Article—Antiochus III; PRIDEAUX, year 217.

10—R
"Antiochus lost upwards of ten thousand foot and three hundred horse, and four thousand of his men were taken prisoners. Philopator, having marched, after his victory, to Jerusalem, was so audacious as to attempt to enter the sanctuary, his heart shall be lifted up; and being returned to his kingdom, he behaved with the upmost pride toward the Jews, and treated them very cruelly. He might have dispossessed Antiochus of his dominions had he taken a proper advantage of his glorious victory; but he contented himself with recovering Coelosyria and Phoenicia, and again plunged into his former excesses; 'but he shall not be strengthened by it.'" ROLLIN, Vol. 4, Page 143.

"Ptolemy (Philopator) having thus regained these provinces, made a progress through them; and, among other cities which he visited in his perambulation, Jerusalem was one that had this favor from him. On his arrival thither, he took a view of the temple, and there offered up many sacrifices to the God of Israel, and made many oblations to the temple, and gave several very valuable donatives to it. But, not being content to view it only from the outer court, beyond which it was not lawful for any gentile to pass, he would have pressed into the sanctuary itself, and into the holy of holies in the temple, where none but the high priest only, once a year, on the great day of expiation, was to enter. This made a great uproar all over the city. The high-priest informed him of the sacredness of the place, and the law of God which forbade his entrance thither. And the priests and Levites gathered together to hinder it, and all the people to deprecate it; and great lamentation was made everywhere among them on the apprehension of the great profanation which would hereby be offered to their holy temple, and all hands were lifted up unto God in prayer to avert it. But the king, the more he was opposed, growing the more intent to have his will in this matter, pressed into the inner court; but, as he was passing farther to go into the temple itself, he was smitten from God with such a terror and confusion of mind, that he was carried out of the place in a manner half dead. On this he departed from Jerusalem, filled with great wrath against the whole nation of the Jews, for that which happened to him in that place, and venting many threatenings against them for it." PRIDEAUX, year 217.

"Ptolemy IV., Philopator ("father-loving"), B. C. 222-205; alluded to in Dan. 11:10-12, defeated Antiochus the Great at Raphia, near Gaza (B. C. 217); sacrificed in the temple, and attempted to enter the sacred precincts, when a shock of paralysis stopped him. He was indolent, effeminate, and licentious, but capable, on occasion, of splendid and vigorous deeds." SCHAFF-HERZOG, Article—Ptolemy IV.

10—S
"Antiochus, after he had ended the war beyond the Euphrates, raised a great army in those provinces. Finding, fourteen years after the conclusion of the first war, that Ptolemy Epiphanes, who was then but five or six years of age, had succeeded Philopator

his father, he united with Philip of Macedon, in order to deprive the infant king of his throne. Having defeated Scopas at Panium, near the source of the river Jordan, he subjected the whole country which Philopator had conquered, by the victory he gained at Raphia." ROLLIN, Vol. 4, page 144.

"He (Antiochus III) then turned towards the eastern frontiers of his realm, against Parthia and Bactria; penetrated into Northern India, and organized a formidable army, including a hundred and fifty Indian elephants. In 204 Philopator died; and the Egyptian crown devolved on his son, Ptolemy V, (Epihanes) a boy of five years. This circumstance Antiochus meant to utilize. He conquered Cocle-Syria, Phoenicia, and Palestine, and gained a decisive victory in 198 at Paneas in Cocle-Syria. Peace was then concluded." SCHAFF-HERZOG. Article—Antiochus III.

"Antiochus, king of Syria, and Philip, king of Macedon, thinking to serve themselves of the advantage they had by the death of Philopator, and the succession of an infant king after him, entered into a league to divide his dominion between them, agreeing that Philip should have Caria, Libya, Cyrene, and Egypt, and Antiochus all the rest. And accordingly Antiochus forthwith marched into Ceole-Syria and Palestine, and partly this year, and partly in the next, made himself master of these provinces, and all the several districts and cities in them." PRIDEAUX, year 203.

"Return of Antiochus from the East, B. C. 205 and resumption of his Egyptian projects. A treaty is made with Philip of Macedon for the partition of the kingdom of Ptolemies between the two powers. War in Ceole-Syria, Phoenicia, and Palestine with varied success, terminated by a great victory over Scopas near Panias, B. C. 198. Marriage of Cleopatra, daughter of Antiochus, with Ptolemy V, (Epiphanes). Cocle-Syria and Palestine promised as a dowry, but not delivered." RAWLINSON, Ancient History, page 254.

10—T
"Antiochus, king of Syria, and Philip, king of Macedon, thinking to serve themselves of the advantage they had by the death of Philopator, and the succession of an infant king after him, entered, into a league to divide his dominions between them." PRIDEAUX, year 203.

"Return of Antiochus from the East, B. C. 205, and resumption of his Egyptian projects. A treaty is made with Philip of Macedon for the partition of the kingdom of the Ptolemies between the two powers." RAWLINSON, Ancient History, page 254.

10—U
"Several apostate Jews, to ingratiate themselves with the king of Egypt, complied with every thing he required of them, even in opposition to the sacred ordinances of the law, by which means they were in great favor with him, but it was of short duration; for, when Antiochus regained possession of Judea and Jerusalem, he either extirpated, or drove out of the country, all the partisans of Ptolemy. This subjugation of the Jews to the sovereignty of the kings of Syria, prepared the way for the accomplishing of the prophecy, which denounced the calamities which Antiochus Epihanes, son of Antiochus the Great, was to bring upon this people; which occasioned a great number of them to fall into apostacy." ROLLIN, Vol. 4, page 144.

"But that he might not seem an enemy to all that nation (the Jews) he ordained, that as many of them as would be initiated into the heathen religion, and sacrifice unto his gods, would retain their former privileges, and remain still in the same rank, which they were of before. But, of the many thousands of the Jewish race which then dwelt at Alexandria, there were found only three hundred who accepted of this condition, and forsook their God to gain the favor of the king. Philopator durst not any longer prosecute his rage against them, but ordered them to be all again set free; (the loyal Jews who had been imprisoned because they would not submit to the king's heathenish orders) and fearing the divine vengeance upon him in their behalf, for the appeasing and diverting of it, he restored them to all their privileges, rescinding and revoking all his decrees which he had published against them; and he added over and above many gifts and favors unto them; among which one was, that he gave them liberty to put to death all those Jews who had apostatized from their religion; which they accordingly executed, not sparing a man of them." PRIDEAUX, year 210

10—V
"At this time (reign of Ptolemy Epiphanes) Antiochus having passed into Lesser Asia, and there engaged himself in a war with Attalus, king of Pergamus, the minister of Alexandria took advantage hereof to send Scopias with an army into Palestine and Coele-Syria, for the recovery of those provinces; where he managed the war with such success that he took several cities, and reduced all Judea by force, and put a garrison into the castle at Jerusalem; and, on the approach of winter, returned to Alexandria with full honor for the victories he had obtained, and with as great riches, which he had gathered from the plunder of the country. . . . The Jews were at this time very much alienated in their affections from the Egyptian king; whether it were by reason of the former ill treatment of their nation by his father, or for some fresher ill usage they had received, is not said. It is most likely it was because of the ravages and robberies of Scopas, on his taking Jerusalem the former year; for he was a very covetous and rapacious man, laying his hands everywhere on all that he could get; and therefore, on Antiochus' marching that way, they willingly Tendered all places unto him, and on his coming to Jerusalem, the priests and elders went out in a solemn procession to meet him, and received him with gladness, and entertained him and all his army in their city, provided for his horses and elephants, and assisted him with their arms for the reducing of the castle; where Scopas had left a garrison. PRIDEAUX, year 198.

"Now it happened that in the reign of Antiochus the Great, who ruled over all Asia, that the Jews, as well as the inhabitants of Cele-syrin, suffered greatly, and their land was sorely harassed; for while be was at war with Ptolemy Philopator, and with his son, who was called Epiphanes, it fell nut that these nations were equally sufferers, both when he was beaten and when he beat the others; so that, they were very like a ship in a storm, which is tossed by the waves on both sides; and just thus were they in their situation in the middle between Antiochus' prosperity and its change to adversity. But at length, when Antiochus had beaten Ptolemy, he seized upon Judea; and when Philopator was dead, his son sent out a great army under Scopas the general of his forces, against the inhabitants of Celesyria, who took many of their cities and in particular our nation; which, when he fell upon them, went over to him. Yet was it not long afterward when Antiochus overcame Scopas, in a battle fought at the fountains of Jordan, and destroyed a great part of his army." Josephus, 12-3-3.

10—W
"Antiochus, having put an end to the war of Coelosyria and Palestine, sent his two sons, at the end of the land-army, to Sardis, while he embarked on board the fleet, and sailed to the Aegean Sea, where lie took several islands, and extended his empire exceedingly on that. side. However, the prince of the people, whom he had insulted by making this invasion, that is L. Scipio, the Roman consul, caused the reproach to turn upon him, by defeating him at Mount Sipilus, and repulsing him from every part of Asia Minor." ROLLIN, Vol. 4, p. 145.

"He (Antiochus III) then invaded Asia Minor, and in 195 he crossed the Hellespont, and advanced into Europe. Here he encountered the Romans; but in 190 he was totally defeated at Magnesia' by Scipio Asiaticus, and he obtained peace from Rome only on very severe conditions." SCHAFF-HERZOG. Article—Antiochus III.

"The conquests of Antiochus in Asia Minor and Europe, B. C. 197 to 196, bring him into contact with the Romans, who require him to evacuate the Chersonese and restore the Greek cities in Asia Minor to freedom. He indignantly rejects their demands, and prepares for war. Flight of Hannibal to his court, B, C. 195. Antiochus makes alliance with the Aetolians, and in B. C. 192 crosses into Greece, lands at Demetrias, takes Chalcis. Great battle at Thermopylae between the Romans, under Aeilius Glabrio, and the allied forces of Antiochus and the Aetolians. Antiochus, completely, defeated, quits Europe and returns to Asia B. C. 191. His fleet has orders to protect the shores and prevent the Romans from landing. But the battle of Corycus ruins these hopes. The Romans obtain the mastery of the sea; and their army, having crossed the Hellespont without opposition, gains under the two Scipios the great victory of Magnesia, which places Antiochus at their mercy, B. C. 190. He purchases peace by ceding all Asia Minor except Cilicia, and by consenting to pay a contribution of 12,000 talents. The ceded provinces are added by the Romans to the kingdom of Pergamus, which is thus raised into a rival to Syria." RAWLINSON Ancient History, page 254. See also MYERS, Ancient History, pp. 290, 291, 430. PRIDEAUX, years 190, 189.

10—X
"Antiochus, after his defeat, returned to Antioch, the capital of his kingdom, and the strongest fortress in it. He went soon after into the provinces of the east, in order to levy money to pay the Romans; but having plundered the temple of Elymais, he there lost his life in a miserable manner." ROLLIN, Vol. 4, page 146.

"The defeat of Magnesia is followed by the revolt of Armenia, B. C. 189, which henceforth becomes independent. It leads also to the death of Antiochus, who, in order to pay the war contribution imposed upon him by the Romans, is driven to the plunder of the Oriental temples. Hence, a tumult in Elymais, wherein the king is killed, B. C. 187." RAWLINSON, Ancient History, page 254.

"Retiring to his eastern provinces in order to raise money for the tribute he (Antiochus III) owed Rome, he was slain in 187, while plundering the temples of Belus in Elymais." SCHAFF-HERZOG. Article—Antiochus III.

10—Y
"These few words (Dan. 11:20) denote, evidently, the short and obscure reign of Seleucus, and the kind of death he was to die. The Hebrew text points him out still more clearly. There shall arise up in his place, 'of Antiochus,' a man who, as an extortioner, a collector of taxes, shall cause to pass away, and shall destroy, the glory of the kingdom.' And, indeed, this was the sole employment of his reign. He was obliged to furnish the Romans, by the articles of peace concluded between them, a thousand talents annually; and the twelve years of this tribute exactly ended with his life. He reigned but eleven years." ROLLIN, Vol. 4, page 203.

"Antiochus was succeeded by his son, Seleucus IV, who took the name of Philopator, and reigned eleven years, B. C. 187 to 176. This period was wholly uneventful. The fear of Rome, and the weakness produced by exhaustion, forced Seleucus to remain quiet, even when Eumenes of Pergamus seemed about to conquer and absorb Pontus. . . . Seleucus was murdered by Heliodorus, his treasurer (B. C. 176), who hoped to succeed to his dominions." RAWLINSON, A. H., page 255.

"After the death of Antiochus the Great, Seleucus Philopator, his eldest son, whom he left at Antioch on his departure thence into the east, succeeded him in the kingdom, but made a very poor figure in it, by reason of the low state which the Romans had reduced the Syrian empire to, and the heavy tribute of one thousand talents a year, which, through the whole time of his reign he was obliged to pay them; by the treaty of peace lately granted by them to his father. The whole of this king's (Seleucus) is expressed by Daniel 11:20. For in that text it is foretold, that after Antiochus the Great, who is spoken of in the foregoing verses, 'there should stand up in his estate a raiser of taxes.' And Seleucus was no more than such all his time, for the whole business of his reign was to raise the thousand talents every year, which, by the treaty of peace that his father had made with the Romans, he was obliged, for twelve years together, and the last of those years was the last of his life. For, as the text saith, that, 'within a few years after he should be destroyed, and that neither in anger, nor in battle'; so accordingly, it happened. For he reigned only eleven years, and his death was neither in battle nor in anger; that is, neither in war abroad, nor in sedition or rebellion at home, but by the secret treachery of one of his own friends. His successor was Antiochus Epiphanes his brother, of whom we shall treat in the next book." PRIDEAUX, years 186, 176.

10—Z
"On the death of Seleucus Philopator, Heliodorus, who had been the treacherous author of his death, endeavored to seize the crown of Syria. Antiochus, the brother of Seleucus, was then on his return from Rome. While at Athens in his journey, he there heard of the death of his brother, and the attempt of Heliodorus to usurp the throne; and finding that the usurper had a great party with him to support him in his pretensions, and that there was another party also forming for Ptolemy, (made some claim to the succession in right of his mother, she being sister to the deceased king) and that both of them were agreed 'not to give unto him (though the next heir in the absence of Demetrius) the honor of the kingdom,' as the holy prophet Daniel foretold, he applied himself to Eumenes, king of Pergamos, and Attalus his brother, and (by flattering speeches and great promises of friendship) prevailed with them to help him against Heliodorus. And by their means that usurper being suppressed, he was quietly placed on the throne, and all submitted to him, and permitted him, without any further opposition, peaceably to obtain the kingdom, as had been predicted of him in the same prophecy. Eumenes and Attalus, at this time having some suspicions of the Romans, were desirous of having the king of Syria on their side, in case a war

should break out between them, and Antiochus' promises to stick by them, whenever such a war should happen, were the inducements that prevailed with them to do him this kindness." PRIDEAUX, year 175. See also, RAWLINSON, A. H., page 255. ROLLIN, Vol. 4, page 204.

11—A
"Heliodorus, the murderer of Seleucus, and his adherents, as also those of the Egyptian king, who had formed designs against Syria, were defeated by the forces of Attalus and Eumenes, dispersed by the arrival of Antiochus, whose presence disconcerted all their projects. By the 'prince of the covenant,' we may suppose to be meant, either Helidorus, the chief of the conspirators, who had killed Seleucus; or rather Ptolemy Epiphanes king of Egypt, Who lost his life by a conspiracy of his own subjects, when he was meditating a war against Syria. Thus, Providence removed this powerful adversary, to make way for Antiochus, and raised him to the throne." ROLLIN, Vol. 4, p 236.

"On the death of Seleucus, the throne was seized by Helidorus; but it was not long before Antiochus, the brother of the late king, with the help of Pergamene monarch, Eumenes, recovered it. This prince, who is known in history as Antiochus IV, or (more commonly) as Antiochus Epiphanes, was a man of courage and energy." RAWLINSON, Ancient History, page 255. See also 10—Z, above.

11—B
"Antiochus, (Epiphanes) though he was already determined on the war, 'yet he shall assume a specious appearance of friendship for the king of Egypt.' He even sent Apollinius to Memphis, to be present at the banquet given on occasion to that prince's coronation, as a proof that it was agreeable to him. But soon after, on pretense of defending his nephew, he marched into Egypt, with a small army, in comparison of those which he levied afterwards. The battle was fought near Peinsum. Antiochus was strongest,

that is, victorious, and afterwards returned to Tyre. Such was the end of his first expedition." ROLLIN, Vol. 4, pages 236, 237.

"Antiochus, having, ever since the return of Apollonius from the Egyptian court, been preparing for the war which he found he must necessarily have with Ptolemy about the provinces of Cocle-Syria and Palestine, and being now ready for it, resolved to defer it no longer—and then forthwith marched his army toward the frontiers of Egypt, where, being met by the forces of Ptolemy (Philometor) between Mount Casius and Pelusium, it there came to a battle between them; in which Antiochus having gotten the victory. . . . without attempting any thing farther this year, returned to Tyre; and there, and in the neighboring cities, put his army into winter quarters." PRIDEAUX, year 171.

11—C

"In these three verses (Dan. 11:24-26) appear the principal characters of the second expedition of Antiochus into Egypt; his mighty armies, his rapid conquests, the rich spoils he curried from thence, and the dissimulation and treachery he began to practice with regard to Ptolemy. Antiochus, after employing the whole winter in making preparations for a second expedition into Egypt, invaded it both by sea and land, as soon as the season would permit. 'Wherefore, he entered into Egypt with a great multitude, with chariots, and elephants, and horsemen, and a great navy. And made war against Ptolemy, king of Egypt; but, Ptolemy was afraid of him, and fled; and many were wounded to death. Thus, they got the strong cities in the land of Egypt, and he took the spoils thereof. 1 Maccab. 1:17, 18, 19. Diodorus relates, that Antiochus, after this victory, conquered all Egypt, or at least the greatest part of it; for all the cities, Alexandria excepted, opened their gates to the conqueror. He subdued Egypt with an astonishing rapidity, and did that 'which his forefathers had not done, nor his fathers' fathers.' Ptolemy either surrendered himself, or fell into the hands of Antiochus, who at first treated him with kindness; had but one table with him; seemed to be greatly concerned for his welfare, and left him the peaceable possession of his kingdom, reserving to himself Pelusium, which was the key' to it. For Antiochus assumed this appearance of friendship, with no other view than to have the better opportunity of ruining him. 'They' that feed of the portion of his meat shall destroy him.' Antiochus did not make a long stay in Egypt at that time, the news which was brought of the general revolt of the Jews, obliging him to march against them. In the meantime, the inhabitants of Alexandria, offended at Philometor for having concluded an alliance with Antiochus, raised Euergetes, his youngest brother, to the throne in his stead. Antiochus, who had advice of what had passed in Alexandria, took the opportunity to return into Egypt, upon pretext of restoring the dethroned monarch, but in reality to make himself absolute master of the kingdom." ROLLIN, Vol. 4, pp. 237, 238.

"Antiochus, having been making preparations during all the winter for a second expedition into Egypt, as soon as the season of the year would permit, again invaded that country both by sea and land. . . . While Antiochus carried on his last invasion, Philometor came into his hands; whether he were taken prisoner by him, or else voluntarily came in unto him, is not said; the latter seems most likely. For Antiochus took not from him his library, but they did eat at the same table, and conversed together as friends; and for some time, Antiochus pretended to take care of the interest of this young king his nephew, and to manage the affairs of the kingdom as tutor and guardian to him. But when he had, under this pretense, made himself master of the country, he seized all to himself; and, having miserably pillaged all parts where he came, vastly enriched himself and his army with the spoils of them." PRIDEAUX, year 171.

11—D
"The third expedition of Antiochus could scarcely be pointed out more clearly. (In Dan. 11:27, 28). That prince, hearing that the Alexandrians had raised Euergetes to the throne, returned to

Egypt upon the specious pretense of restoring Philometer. After having overcome the Alexandrians in a sea fight at Pelusium, he laid siege to Alexandria. But, finding the inhabitants made a strong opposition, he was contented with making himself master of Egypt again, in the name of his nephew, in whose defense he pretended to have drawn the sword. They were then at Memphis, ate at the same table, and behaved towards one another with all the outward marks of a sincere friendship. The uncle seemed to have the nephew's interest at heart, and the nephew to repose the highest confidence in his uncle; but all this was mere show, both dissembling their real sentiments. The uncle endeavored to crush his nephew, and the nephew, who saw through his design, strove immediately to be reconciled to his brother. Thus neither succeeded in deceiving the other; nothing was yet determined, and Antiochus returned into Syria." ROLLIN, Vol. 4, page 239.

"Antiochus, on hearing of this (the raising of Euergetes to throne of Egypt) laid hold of the occasion for his making of a third expedition into Egypt, under pretence of restoring the deposed king, but in reality, to subject the whole kingdom to himself. Ptolemy Euergetes and Cleopatra his sister, who were then shut up in the town, being hereby much distressed, sent ambassadors to the Romans to represent their case, and pray relief. And, a little after there came ambassadors from the Rhodians, to endeavor to make peace between the two kings. But while they were proceeding in long harangues on these topics, Antiochus interrupted them, and in few words told them that there was no need of long orations as to this matter; that the kingdom belonged to Philometor the elder brother, with whom he had some time since made peace, and was now in perfect friendship with him; that, if they would recall him from banishment, and again restore him to his crown, the war would be at an end. This said he, not that he intended any such thing, but only out of craft farther to embroil the kingdom, for the better obtaining of his own ends upon it. . . . And, with this view having withdrawn from Alexandria, he marched to Memphis, and there seemingly again restored the whole kingdom to Philometer, excepting only Pelusium, which he retained in his hands, that, having this key of Egypt still in his keeping, he might thereby again enter Egypt, when matters should there, according to the scheme which he had laid, be ripe for it, and so seize the whole kingdom; and, having thus disposed matters, he returned again to Antioch," PRIDEAUX, year 169.

11—E
"Fourth Expedition of Antiochus into Egypt—Advice being brought to Antiochus, that the two brothers were reconciled, he threw off the mask, and declared publicly that he intended to conquer Egypt for himself. And, to support his pretensions, 'he returned toward the south,' that is, into Egypt, but was not so successful in this expedition as before. As he was advancing to besiege Alexandria, Popilius and the other Roman ambassadors, who were on board a fleet composed of Macedonian or Greek ships, for this the Hebrew word Chittim signifies, which they found at Delos, obliged him to lay down his arms, and leave Egypt. He obeyed, but 'with the utmost reluctance, and made the city and temple of Jerusalem feel the dire effects of his indignation,' as will be presently seen." ROLLIN, Vol. 4, pages 239, 240. See also PRIDEAUX, years 169, 168.

11—F
"After this, having spoiled the city of all its riches, they (forces of Epiphanes) set it on fire in several places, demolished the houses, and pulled down the walls round about it; and then, with the ruins of the demolished city, built a strong fortress on the top of an eminence in the city of David, which was over against the temple; and overlooked and commanded the same, and there placed a strong garrison; and making it a place of arms against the whole nation of the Jews, stored it with all manner of provisions of war, and there also they laid up the spoils which they had taken in the sacking of the city. And this fortress, by the advantage of its situation, being thus higher than the mountain of the temple, and commanding the same, from thence the garrison soldiers fell on

all those that went up thither to worship, and shed their blood on every side of the sanctuary, and defiled it with all manner of pollutions; so that from this time the temple became deserted, and the daily sacrifices ommitted; and none of the true servants of God durst any more go up thither to the worship, till Judas, after three years and a half, having recovered it out of the hands of the heathens, purged the place of its pollutions, and, by a new dedication, restored it again to its pristine use." PRIDEAUX, year 168.

11—G
"Mattathias and Judas Maccabeus supported the distressed nation, and the almost universally abandoned religion, with so small a number of forces, that we can consider the success which the Almighty gave their arms no otherwise than a miracle. The troops grew more numerous by degrees, and afterwards formed a very considerable body." ROLLIN, Vol. 4, page 242.

"At this time Judas Maccabaeus, with some others that accompanied him, fled into the wilderness, and there lived in great hardship, subsisting themselves upon herbs, and what else the mountains and woods could afford them, till they gained an opportunity of taking up arms for themselves and their country, in manner as will be hereafter related." PRIDEAUX, year 168.

"These measures (of Epiphanes) induced an open revolt, whose leader was the priest and patriot Mattathias of Modin. His bold deed of the public murder of a royal official was the sign for the beginning of the revolt. Fleeing to the mountains, he, with the cooperation of his five heroic sons, organized war on a small scale. He died 166 B. C." SCHAFF-HERZOG. Article—Maccabees.

11—H
"Epiphanes ridiculed all religions. He plundered the temples of Greece, and wanted to rob that of Elytnais. He exercised his impious fury chiefly against Jerusalem and the Jews, and almost

without resistance. The Almighty seemed to wink for a time at all the abominations which were committed in his temple, till his wrath against his people was satisfied," ROLLIN, Vol. 4, page 242.

"Meanwhile Antiochus met with very little success in the East. He attempted to plunder the rich temple of Nanaea in Elymais, but was repelled by the inhabitants, and died shortly after (164) at Taba, having just received the news from Judea." SCHAFF-HERZOG. Article—Antiochus IV.

11—I
"On his being thus settled on the throne, he took the name of Epiphanes, that is, The Illustrious; but nothing could be more alien to his true character than this title. The prophet Daniel foretold of him that he would be 'a vile person,' so our English version hath it; but the word nibzeh in the original rather signified despicable than vile. He was truly both in all that both these words can express, which will fully appear from the character given him by Polybius, 11, Philarchus, 12, Livy, 13, and Diodorus Siculus, 14, who were all heathen writers, and the two first of them his contemporaries. For they tell us, that he would get often out of the palace and ramble about the streets of Antioch, with two or three servants only accompanying him; that he would be often conversing with those that graved in silver, and cast vessels of gold, and be frequently found with them in their shops, talking and nicely arguing with them about the mysteries of their trades, that he would very commonly debase himself to the meanest company, and on his going abroad would join in with such as he happened to find them met together, although of the lowest of the people, and enter into discourse with any of them whom he should first fight on; that he would, in his rambles, frequently drink with strangers and foreigners, and even with the meanest and vilest of them; that, when he heard of any young company met together to feast, drink, or any otherwise to make merry together, he would, without giving any notice of his own coming,

intrude himself among them, and revel away the time with them in their cups and songs, and other frolics, without any regard to common decency, or his own royal character, so that several, being surprised with the strangeness of the thing, would, on his coming, get up and run away cut of the company. And he would sometimes, as the freak took him, lay aside his royal habit, and putting on a Roman gown, go round the city, as he had seen done in the election of the magistrates of Rome, and ask the votes of the citizens, in the same manner as used to be there practiced, now taking one man by the hand, and, then embracing another, and would thus set himself up, sometimes for the office of aedile, and sometimes for that of tribune; and, having been thus voted into office he sued for, he would take the cruel chair, and sitting down in it, hear petty causes of contracts, bargains, and sales, made in the market, and give judgment in them with that serious attention and earnestness, as if they had been matters of the highest concern and importance. It is said also of him, that he was much given to drunkenness; and that he spent a great part of his revenues in reveling and drunken carousals; and would often go out into the streets while in these frolics, and there scatter his money by handfuls among the rabble, crying out, 'Let him take to whom fortune gives it.' Sometimes he would go abroad with a crown of roses upon his head, and wearing a Roman gown, would walk the streets alone, and carrying stones under his arms, would throw them at those who followed after him. And he would often wash himself in the public baths among the common people, and there expose himself by many absurd and ridiculous actions. Which odd and extravagant, sort of conduct made many doubt how the matter stood with him; some thinking him a fool, and some a madman; the latter of these, most thought to be his truest character; and therefore, instead of Epiphanes, or the Illustrious, they called him Epimanes, the Madman. Jerome tells us also of him that he was exceedingly given to lasciviousness, and often by the vilest acts of it debased the honor of his royal dignity; that he was frequently found in the company of mimics, pathics, and common prostitutes, and that with the latter he would commit acts of lasciviousness, and gratify his lust on them publicly in the sight of the people. And it is further related of him, that having for his catamites two vile persons, called Timarchus and Heralides, who were brothers, he made the first of them governor of Babylonia, and the other his treasurer in that province, and gave himself up to be governed and conducted by them in most that he did. And having, on a very whimsical occasion, exhibited games and shows at Daphne, near Antioch, with vast expense, and called thither a great multitude of people from foreign parts, as well as from his own dominion, to be present at the solemnity; he there behaved himself to that degree of folly and absurdity, as to become the ridicule and scorn of all that were present; which actions of his are sufficiently abundant to demonstrate him both despicable and vile, though he had not added to them that most unreasonable and wicked persecution of God's people in Judaea and Jerusalem; which will be hereafter related." PRIDEAUX, year 175. See also RAWLINSON, A. H., page 255. ROLLIN, Vol. 4, pages 118-237. SCHAFF-HERZOG, Article—Antiochus IV.

11—J

"On his arrival thither, (Epiphanes at Ecbatana in Media) greatly grieved for this baffle and disappointment at Elymais, news came to him of what happened to Nicanor and Timotheus in Judea; at which being exceedingly enraged, he hastened back, with all the speed he was able, to execute the utmost of his wrath upon the people of the Jews, breathing nothing else but threats of utter destruction and utter extirpation against them all the way as he went. As he was thus hastening toward the country of Babylonia, through which he was to pass in his return, he met on the road the other messengers, which brought him an account how the Jews had defeated Lysias, recovered the temple of Jerusalem, pulled down the images and altars which he had there greeted, and restored that place to its former worship; at which being enraged to the utmost fury, he commanded his charioteer to double his speed, that he might be the sooner on the place to execute his revenge upon the people, threatening, as he went, that he would make Jerusalem a place of sepulture for the Jews, wherein he would bury the whole nation, destroying them all to a man. But while these proud words were in his mouth, the judgment of God overtook him; for he had no sooner spoken them, but he was smitten with an incurable plague, a great pain seizing his bowels, and a grievous torment following thereupon in his inward parts, which no remedy could abate. However, he would not slacken his speed; but still continuing in the same wrath, he drove on the same haste to execute it, till at length, his chariot overthrowing, he was cast to the ground with such violence, that he was sorely bruised and hurt in all the members of his body; whereon he was put into a litter; but not being able to bear that, he was forced to put in at a town called Tabae, lying in the mountains of Paractacene, in the confines of Persia and Babylonia, and there betake himself to his bed, where he suffered horrid torments both in mind and body. For in his body a filthy ulcer broke out in his secret parts, wherein were bred an innumerable quantity of vermin continually flowing from it; and such a stench proceeding from the same, as neither those that attended him nor he himself could well bear; and in this condition he lay languishing and rotting till he died. And all this while the torments of his mind were as great as the torments of his body, caused by the reflections which he made on his former actions. Polybius tells us of this, as well as Josephus, and the authors of the first and second books of Maccabees; and adds hereto, that it grew so far upon him as to come to a constant delirium, or state of madness, by reason of several specters and apparitions of evil spirits, which he imagined were continually about him, reproaching and stinging his conscience with accusations of his past evil deeds which he had been guilty of. Polybius saith, this was for the sacrilegious attempt which he made upon the temple of Diana in Elymais, overlooking that which he had actually executed upon the temple at Jerusalem. Josephus reproves him for this, and with much more reason and justice, lays the whole cause of his suffering in this sickness, as did Antiochus himself, to what he did at Jerusalem, and the temple of God in that place, and the horrid persecution which he thereon raised against all that worshipped him there." PRIDEAUX, year 164.

11—K
"The Kingdom of Israel (953-722 B.C.).—The kingdom of the Ten Tribes maintained its existence for about two hundred years. Many passages of its history are recitals of the struggles between the worship of the national god Yahweh (Jehovah) and the idolatrous service of the gods of the surrounding nations. The cause of Yahweh was boldly espoused by a line of remarkable prophets, among whom Elijah and Elisha in the ninth century, and Amos and Hosea in the eighth, stand preeminent.

"The little kingdom was at last overwhelmed by the Assyrian power in the history of Assyria, was captured by Sargon, king of Ninevah, and the flower of the people were carried away into captivity beyond the Mesopotamian rivers.

"The gaps made in the population of Samaria by the deportation of its best inhabitants were filled with other subjects or captives of the Assyrian king. The descendants of these, mingled with the Israelites that were still left in the country, formed the Samaritans of the time of Christ.

The Kingdom of Judah (531-586 B. C.). This little kingdom, torn by internal religious dissensions, and often on the very verge of ruin from Egyptian or Assyrian armies, maintained an independent existence for over three centuries. But upon the extension of the power of Babylon to the west, Jerusalem was forced to acknowledge the suzerainty of the Babylonian kings.

"The kingdom at last shared the fate of its northern rival. Nebuchadnezzar, the powerful king of Babylon, in revenge for an uprising of the Jews, besieged and captured Jerusalem and carried away a large part of the people into captivity at Babylon. This event virtually ended the separate political life of the Hebrew race (586 B. C.)." Myers' Ancient History, pages 78, 79.

"And such was the end of the nation of the Hebrews, as it hath been delivered down to us, it having twice gone beyond Euphrates; for; the people of the ten tribes were carried out of Samaria by the Assyrians' in the days of king Hoshea; after which the people of the two tribes that remained after Jerusalem was taken were carried away by Nebuchadnezzar, the king of Babylon and Chaldea. Now as to Shalmanezer, he removed the Israelites out of their country, and placed therein the nations of the Cutheans, who had formerly belonged to the inner parts of Persia and Media, but were then called Samaritans, by taking the name of the country to which they were removed: but the king of Babylon, who brought out the two tribes, placed no other nation in their country, by which means all Judea and Jerusalem, and the temple; continued to be a desert for seventy years; but the entire interval of time which passed from the captivity of the Israelites, (the 10 tribes) to the carrying away of the two tribes proved to be a hundred and thirty years, six months, and ten days." Josephus, Antiquities, Book 10, Chapter 9, Section 7.

11—L
"Kings, First and Second Books of—Sources of information. There was a regular series of state annals for both the kingdom of Judah and that of Israel, which embraced the whole time comprehended in the books of Kings, or at least to the end of the reign of Jehoiakim. 2 Kings 24:5. These annals are constantly cited by name as 'the book of the acts of Solomon,' 1 Kings 11:41; and after Solomon 'the book of the Chronicles of the Kings of Judah' or 'Israel,' e. g. 1 Kings 14:29; 15:7; 16:5, 14:20; 2 Kings 10:34; 24:5, etc.; and it is manifest that the author of Kings had them both before him while he drew up his history, in which the reigns of the two kingdoms are harmonized and these annals constantly appealed to. But in addition to these national annals, there were also extant, at the time that the books of Kings

were compiled, separate works of the several prophets who had lived in Judah and Israel."

"Chronicles, First and Second Books of—As regards the materials used by Ezra, they are not difficult to discover. The genealogies are obviously transcribed from some register, in which were preserved the genealogies of the tribes and families drawn up at different times; while the history is mainly drawn from the same documents as those in the book of Kings." (See above) SMITH'S BIBLE DICTIONARY, pp. 336, 116.

ALPHABETICAL INDEX

Acts 17:21 verified	6—A
Acts 23:5, side lights on	5—Q
Adam, meaning of the word	2—G
Adventists	8—P
Age of Christ historical (not mythological) one	5—L
Ahasuerus, identity	8—D
Alexander's flying trip	1—Y
Alexander's four successors	2—A
Alexander's successors; included others besides the "four" noted ones,	10—L
Alexander; did he "sigh for more worlds" etc?	10—H
Alexander; Eusebius' estimate of	7—U
Alexander, none as strong	1—Z
Alexander and Ptolemies in Egypt	5—T
Alexander and Tyre	3—D
Alexander is shown prophecy of Daniel	9—M
Alexander Mack, and the "Brethren" or Dunkards	4—G
All disciples did not follow apostasy	7—K
Altar built at Egypt	1—M
Altar to unknown God	6—B
Ancient government of the Church gone	4—P
Ancients not Sabbath keepers	7—K
Animals, Egypt worshipped	2—P
Antioch, Alexandria, Rome and Constantinople, promin	4—Q
Antiochus III., the Great, attacks Egypt	10—P
Antiochus III. returns against Egypt; stronger	10—S
Antiochus invades Europe; defeated by Romans	10—W
Antiochus' disgraceful death	10—X
Aramea distinguished from Syria proper	6—J
Arianism	7—1,

Arabians circumcise at 13th year	2—J
Arabians, Ishmael founder of…	1—E
Artaxerxes' treatment of the women	1—I
Asphaltitis, lake, or Dead Sea	3—T
Assyrian and Babylonian captivity	11—K
Assyrian Empire, rise of…	1—S
Babel, tower of, heathen account	5—K
Babylon, Cyrus enters after diverting river	8—G
Babylon, destruction of city	2—Y
Babylon, fall of	1—W
Babylon, later city of	6—B
Babylon, rivers and willows	6—L
Babylon, the greatest city of all	8—H
Babylon, walls and gates of ancient	2—Q
Babylonian and Assyrian captivity	11—K
Babylonian Empire, early	1—B
Babylonian Empire, later	1—T
Babylonians and Assyrians, why same "from north"	5—S
Bacchus, feast of	2—Z
Bad effects of absence of capital punishment	7—W
Balaam's counsel to Midianites and Moabites	3—F
Banks of Jordan	6—G
Baptism of infants	8—W
Baptist, John	3—L
Baptists	8—Q
Baptists, Calvinistic, Calvin and	4—B
Bartholomew's Day, Saint, massacre of	9—E
Beating with stripes	6—V
Beginning date, new moon as	5—O
Beginning of Councils	1—N
Belshazzar and his father, joint rule	5—O
Belshazzar and Nebuchadnezzar	8—A
Berenice, daughter of Philadelphus, marries Antiochus	10—M
Bible and democracy (quote from Atlantic Monthly)	9—S
Birth of Christ, date uncertain	10—A and 5—A
Birth stools	6—K

Bishop, original power of	4—K
Bishop, power increased	4—L
Bishops, power further increased	4—Z
Books of Bible, concerning titles	5—N
Books of Old Testament, compiling	6—E
Bowels, seat of passions, ancient theory	8—H
Brass, Greeks used arms of	2—D
Bread and wine of communion	6—Z
"Brethren" or Dunkards	4—G
Brevity of human existence, Gibbon	10—B
Brief of church government, taken from Mosheim	10—C
Brown and Brownists or Congregationalists	4—F
Calvin and Calvinistic Baptists	4—B
Canoes, papyrus	5—X
Canons of Old and New Testaments, time between	5—Z
Captivity cured Jews of idolatry	5—R
Cestius' unaccountable retreat	2—T
Christ, age, historical (not mythological) one	5—L
Christ, date of birth uncertain	5—A
Christ, Josephus' testimony concerning	3—K
Chronological table of dates	5—I
Church and State	4—U
Church and State united by Constantine	4—Y
Church of England; Henry VIII	4—H
Churches, early, independent	4—J
Circumcise 13th year, Arabians	2—J
Circumcision disguised	1—L
Civil rulers, power of pope over.	4—W
Climax power of the pope	4—V
Commandments, the ten	1—F
Concentration of power	4—M
Concentration of power, further	4—O
Concerning John the Baptist	3—L
Concerning titles, books of Bible	6—N
Condition of France during Revolution	5—P
Confessional, private, origin	5—C

Congregationalists; Brown and Brownists	4—F
Constantine and Sunday	7—V and 5—D
Constantine "takes away" Pagan Rome	4—X
Constantine unites Church and State	4—Y
Constantinople, and others, prominence	4—Q
Convent, first female	5—F
Councils, beginning of	4—N
Counsel of Balaam	3—F
Curious feature of ancient irrigation	5—W
Curse upon the serpent	2—H
Compiling books of Old Testament	6—E
Cyrus, and Darius the Mede	6—M
Christian Era	10—A and 6—N
Chronology, note on	6—P
Contribution every Sunday	6—Y
Communion, bread and wine for	6—Z
Church letters	7—B
Church and State, separation, not thought of by the Reformers	7—D
Council of Nice	7—G
Consubstantial? or like—substance	7—H
Christ's ministry, length of it	7—Q
Cross, famous vision of	7—T
Capital punishment	7—W
Canon of Old and New Testaments	8—O and 7—Z
Commercial importance of Phoenicia	8—B
Cyrus diverts Euphrates and enters Babylon	8—G
Canon of Bible and the "Church"	8—O
Catholic Church, first mention of	8—O
Cyrenius sent to tax the Jews	9—R
Choirs	9—U and 9—W
Congregational singing	9—U and 9—W
Christmas	10—F
Captivity, Babylonian and Assyrian	1—K
Daily sacrifice congregational	1—G
Date of first-fruits	1—H

Difference, Pharisees and Sadusees	1—X
Date of Josephus' birth; his three sons	2—L
Daily-sacrifice stopped by Epiphanes	2—R
Death of Epiphanes, miraculous	2—S
Distress of siege of Jerusalem	2—W
Distraction of city of Babylon	2—Y
Disease of Herod	3—1
Dying, wicked designs of Herod	3—J
Death, violent, of Herod Agrippa	3—M
Dead Sea, or Lake Asphaltitis	3—T
Denmark, Frederick in	4—A
Dunkards and Alexander Mack	4—G
Date of Christ's birth uncertain	5—A
Dates, various, for ascension of Menes	5—H
Dates, chronological table of	5—I
Deluge, heathen account of	5—J
Darius the Mede, and Cyrus	6—M
Date, begun by new moon	6—S
Difference, enchanters and preachers	7—A
Death of Apostle John	7—F
Disciples, not all followed apostacy	7—K
"Defence" second, of Paul	7—M
Division of Roman Empire into East and West	8—J
Democracy and the Bible (quote Atlantic Monthly)	9—S
Dionysius Exiguus and the Christian Era	10—A
Early-Babylonian Empire	1—R
"Egypt, River of"	2—E
Egyptian; mid-wives were	2—I
Espousal and marriage	2—N
Egyptians worshipped animals	2—P
Epiphanes stopped daily sacrifice	2—R
Eagle, the Roman	2—U
Egypt; Nebuchadnezzar subdues	3—B
Engines of Romans, violence	3—Q
"Even with the ground," Jerusalem laid	3—X
Early churches independent	4—J

178 | Historical Quotations

Evolution turned round; The Weddas	5—G
Egypt, Alexander and Ptolemies rule in	5—T
Egyptians and Ethiopians taken by Sennacharib	5—V
Ethiopians and Egyptians taken by Sennacharib	5—V
Eats son in a siege, a mother	5—Y
Era, the Christian	10—A and 6—N
Explanatory note on chronology	6—P
Ebionism	7—X and 6—U
Every Sunday, contribution	6—Y
Enchanters and preachers, difference	7—A
Eusebius' estimate of Alexander	7—U
Edict of Constantine for Lord's Day	5—D and 7—V
Eusebius' description of Ebionis	7—X
Egypt, length of Israelites' sojourn in	5—F
Euphrates, Cyrus diverts, and enters Babylon	8—G
East and West, Roman Empire divided into	8—J
Eastern and Western Churches	8—K
Episcopal Church, Protestant, in America	8—U
Episcopalians, or, Episcopal Church	8—U
Earthquake in days of Uzziah	9—L
Epiphanes desecrates the worship	9—N
Epiphanes; date of his desecration of worship	9—O
Easter	10—G
Epiphanes' forces desecrate the worship	11—F
Epiphanes; first expedition against Egypt	11—B
Epiphanes; second expedition against Egypt	11—C
Epiphanes; third expedition against Egypt	11—D
Epiphanes; fourth expedition against Egypt	11—E
Epiphanes' manner of obtaining the crown	10—Z
Epiphanes overcomes the usurper and his friends	11—A
Epiphanes' attitude toward religion	11—11
Epiphanes' vile and despicable character	11—1
Epiphanes' terrible death	11—J
First-fruits, date	1—I
Fall of Babylon	1—W
"Flying trip" of Alexander	1—Y

Four successors of Alexander	2—A
First-fruits, offering of	2—M
Fig tree, the	2—V
Feast of Bacchus	2—Z
Fall of Ninevah	3—A
Fredrick in Denmark	4—A
Fox and the Quakers	4—E
Further concentration of power	4—O
Form of government patriarchal	4—R
Female convent, first	5—F
France, condition during Revolution	5—P
Fusion of races, Ptolemy effects	5—U
Famous vision of the cross	7—T
Gods, Mesopotamians carry when traveling	1—A
Gauls, Medes and Greeks, origin	1—C
Greeks, Gauls & Medes, origin	1—C
Greeks used arms of brass	2—D
Gates and walls of Ancient Babylon	2—Q
Grief of Herod for his wife	3—H
Greatest misfortunes of all times, Jerusalem	3—O
Galilee or Gennesareth, Sea of	3—S
Gennesareth or Galilee, Sea of	3—S
Government, patriarchal form of	4—R
General persecutions, ten	6—10
Great Synagogue	6—S
Grecians	7—E
Greeks received letters from Phoenicia	8—C
Government, Jewish (under Romans) in Palestine	8—E
Greek and Roman Churches	8—K
Gauls thought human sacrifices necessary	8—N
Greek Church older and source of Roman	9—X
Government of Church; a brief taken from Masheim	10—C
Gentile permitted to offer sacrifice	10—R
Hebrew, origin of the word	1—D
Herod succeeds Maccabees	1—P
High priests, order in which they served	2—O

Herod's nationality	3—G
Herod's grief for his wife	3—H
Herod's terrible disease	3—I
Herod's dying wicked designs	3—J
Herod Agrippa's violent death	3—M
High priests; order, service and regulations	3—N
Heb, 11:27. An illustration	3—P
Henry VIII and Church of England	4—H
Heathen account of deluge	5—J
Heathen account of tower of Babel	5—K
Historical one, age of Christ	5—L
Herod, nationality and religion	6—X
Horrible persecutions of Pagans	7—I
Head downward, Peter crucified	7—N
Hebrew; Matthew written	7—Z and 7—S
Human sacrifice necessary, Gauls thought	8—N
Herod; date when he became King of the Jews	9—Q
Ishmael, founder of Arabians	1—E
Iron-like strength of Roman Empire	2—C
Illustration of Heb. 11:37	3—P
Independent, early churches were	4—J
Increased, power of bishop	4—L
Increased, papal authority	4—T
Illustration last part Romans 1st chapter	5—B
Idolatry, captivity cured Jews of	5—R
Irrigation, curious feature of ancient	5—W
Idolaters, Samaritans were not	6—Q
Infalibility of popes	7—C
Ignatious' words on his martyrdom	7—O
Importance of Phoenicia as to commerce	8—B
Identity of Ahasuerus	8—D
Israelites in Egypt; how long?	8—F
Illustration of John 3:8	8—M
Infant baptism	8—W
Instrumental music in worship	9—V and 8—X
I. H. S	9—B

I. N. E. I	9—C
Inscription on fence around Friend's Church	9—G
Idumeans receive circumcision and become Jews	9—P
Image worship—Greeks and Roman churches	9—Y
Jerusalem, pools in	1—B
Jews, many, carried into Egypt	1—J
Jerusalem—Pompey takes	1—P
Jerusalem, unlawful to kill out of	1—Q
Josephus of priestly family	2—F
Josephus, date of his birth	2—L
Jerusalem, siege, distress in	2—W
Jerusalem, sedition in	2—X
Josephus' testimony concerning Christ	3—K
John the Baptist	3—L
Jerusalem, misfortunes greatest of all times	3—O
Jerusalem, why such vast numbers present, siege	3—IT
Jews, many for sale, but few (or none) to buy.	3—W
Jerusalem laid "even with the ground"	3—X
Joint rule Belshazzar and his father	5—0
Jews cured of idolatry after captivity	5—R
Jordan, thickets and banks	6—G
John, apostle, death of…	7—F
Jewish government (under Romans) in Palestine	8—E
John 3:18 illustrataed	8—M
Jerusalem, siege of, Christians departed before	9—1
Jews' apostatized—selfish motive failed	10—T
Kill out of Jerusalem, unlawful	1—Q
Kinship, origin, Medes and Persians	1—U
Kings and Chronicles, books of, sources	11—L
Kings, the Shepherd	2—K
Knox and Presbyterianism	4—0
Later Babylonian Empire	1—T
Laid "even with the ground" Jerusalem	3—X
Luther and Lutheranism	3—Y
Later city of Babylon	6—E
Letters, church	7—B

Like substance? or Consubstantial?	7—H
Length of Christ's ministry	7—Q
Lord's day, edict of Constantine	5—D and 7—V
Letters, Greeks received from Phoenicia	8—C
Length of sojourn in Egypt, Israelites	8—F
Latin and Greek or Eastern Churches	8—K
Mesopotamians carry their gods while traveling	1—A
Medes, Gauls and Greeks, origin	1—C
Many Jews carried into Egypt	1—J
Maccabees, period of	1—O
Maccabees, Herod succeeds	1—P
Medes and Persians, origin and kinship	1—U
Medo-Persian Empire, origin	1—V
Medes at first in lead	1—X
Meaning of the word "Adam"	3—G
Maccabees; "small," "little" forces at start	11—G
Order, service and regulations of High Priests	3—N
Original power of Bishop	4—K
Origin of private confessional	5—O
Original day of worship, Sunday	5—E
Old and New Testament, time between canons	5—Z
Old Testament canon complied	7—Z and 6—S
Old and New Testament canon	6—S and 7—Z
Organs	6—X and 9—V
Pools in Jerusalem	1—B
Pharisees and Sadusees, one difference	1—N
Period of the Maccabees	1—O
Pompey takes Jerusalem	1—P
Persians and Medes, origin and kinship	1—U
Persian Empire, Medo, origin	1—V
Priestly family, Josephus of	2—F
Petri in Sweden	3—Z
Presbyterianism and Knox	4—C
Power of bishop, original	4—K
Power of bishop, increased	4—L
Power, concentration of	4—M

Power, further concentration of...	4—O
Prominence, Rome, Antioch, Alexandria, Constantinople	4—Q
Patriarchal form of government	4—R
Papal authority increased	4—T
Pope, climax of his authority	4—V
Power of pope over civil rulers..	4—W
Pope, his power over civil rulers	4—W
Pagan Rome "taken away" by Constantine	4—X
Power of prominent bishops further increased	4—Z
Private confessional, origin	5—C
Pliny-Trajan correspondence about Christians	5—M
Ptolemies rule in Egypt.	5—T
Ptolemy effects fusion of the races	5—U
Papyrus canoes of Egypt and Ethiopia	5—X
Persecutions, ten general	6—F
Passions; bowels seat of, ancient theory	6—H
Proselytes	6—T
Preachers and enchanters, difference	7—A
Popes, infallibility	7—C
Persecutions, horrible, by pagans	7—I
Paul's second "defense"	7—M
Paul and Peter; martyrdom	7—M and 7—N
Peter and Paul; martyrdom	7—M and 7—N
Peter crucified head downward	7—N
Polycarp, noted words	7—P
Punishment, capital, bad effects of absence	7—W
Phoenicia, commercial importance of	8—B
Phoenicia, gave letters to Greeks	8—C
Palestine, Jewish government, under Romans	8—E
Pope	8—L
Protestant Episcopal Church in America	8—U
Peter; was he ever in Rome?	7—Y
Protestant, origin of the word	9—D
Ptolemy III, Euergetes, comes against Syria	10—N
Ptolemy III recovers idols of Egypt	10—O
Ptolemy Philopator defeats Antiochus III	10—Q

184 | *Historical Quotations*

Ptolemy Philopator, his pride and arrogance	10—R
Ptolemy V. League formed to "stand" against him	10—T
Quakers, the, and Fox	4—E
Rise of Assyrian Empire	1—8
Roman Empire; iron—like strength	2—C
"River of Egypt"	2—E
Retreat, Cestius' unaccountable	2—T
Roman eagle, the…	2—U
Roman engines, violence	3—Q
Reference to hired mourners	3—R
"Reformed Church" and Zuingli	4—D
Rome, Antioch, Alexandria, Constant., prominence	4—Q
Rome, supremacy, introduced	4—S
Relation of Church and State	4—U
Rulers, civil, power of pope over	4—W
Rome, Pagan, "Taken away" by Constantine	4—X
Romans 1st chapter, illustration of last part	5—R
Rule of Alexander and Ptolemies in Egypt	5—T
Races, Ptolemy effects fusion of…	5—U
Regulations for transcribers	6—C
Rivers and willows of Babylon	6—L
Reformers, not think of separation, church and state	7—D
Rome, was Peter ever in?	7—Y
Romans, and Jewish government in Palestine	8—E
Roman Empire, divided, into East and West	8—J
Roman and Greek churches	8—K
Rome on seven hills	9—H
Reclining, position while eating	9—J
Religious state of world at advent of Christ	9—K
Religion destroyed by science	9—T
Robbers of the Jews repulsed	10—Q
Sacrifice, daily, congregational	1—G
Septuagent, origin	1—K
Sadusees and Pharisees; the difference	1—N
Strong as Alexander, none as	1—Z
Successors, Alexander's four	2—A

Strength of Roman Empire	2—C
Shepherd kings	2—K
Sons of Josephus	2—L
Sacrifice, daily, Epiphanes stops	2—B
Siege of Jerusalem; distress	2—W
Sedition in Jerusalem	2—X
Service of High Priests	3—N
Sea of Galilee or Gennesareth	3—8
Sea, Dead, or Lake Asphaltitis	3—T
Siege of Jerusalem, why such vast numbers	3—U
"Sacrifice and oblation" cease	3—V
Sale, Jews; but few to buy	3—W
Sweden, Petri in	3—Z
Supremacy of Rome introduced	4—S
State and Church, relation	4—U
Supreme control of church, Constantine assumes, and unites Church and State	4—Y
Sunday, Constantine and	7—V and 5—D
Sunday original day of worship	5—E
Side lights on Acts 23:5	5—Q
Sennacharib takes Egyptians and Ethiopians	5—V
Son, mother eats in siege	5—Y
Statement in Acts 17:21 verified	6—A
Statement in Neh. 8:8 illustrated	6—D
Seat of passions in bowels, ancient theory	6—H
Syria (or Aramea) distinguished from Syria proper	6—J
Stools, birth	6—K
Samaritans not idolaters	6—Q
Synagogue, Great	6—S
Stripes, beating with	6—V
Souls, transmigration of	6—W
Sunday, contribution every	6—Y
Separation, Church and State, not thought of by Reformers	7—D
Scriptures no longer authority	7—J
Second "defence" of Paul...	7—M
Sabbath keepers, ancients not	7—R

186 | *Historical Quotations*

Sojourn in Egypt of Israelites, how long?	8—F
Sacrifice, human, thought necessary by Gauls	8—N
Sprinkling, and pouring	8—V
Sabbath—Day's journey	8—Y
Sunday—Schools; modern	8—Z
Salvation Army	9—A
Seven hills of Rome	9—H
Siege of Jerusalem, Christians departed before	9—I
Science destroyed by religion (Atlantic Monthly)	9—T
Singing of primitive church	9—U and 9—W
Selections, "raiser of taxes"	10—Y
Ten commandments	1—F
Treatment of women, Artaxerxes'	1—I
Tyre and Nebuchadnezzar	3—C
Tyre and Alexander	3—D
"Taken away" pagan Rome, by Constantine....	.4—X
Table of dates, chronological	5—1
Tower of Babel, heathen account	5—K
Trajan—Pliny, correspondence about Christians	5—M
Titles, books of Bible, concerning	5—N
Time between canons of Old and New Testaments	5—Z
Transcribers, regulations for	6—C
Ten general persecutions	6—F
Thickets and banks of Jordan	6—G
Thebes, or No, in Egypt, captured	6—I
Transmigration of souls	6—W
Tarsus, its riches and importance	8—1
Tiberius shares throne with Augustus	9—R
Twelve hundred years Constantine to Reformation	9—Z
Unlawful to kill out of Jerusalem	1—Q
Unaccountable retreat of Cestius	2—T
Union, Church and State under Constantine	4—Y
Unknown God, altar to	6—B
Universalists	8—T
Uzziah offering incense; earthquake	9—L
Violence of Roman engines	3—Q

Violent death, Herod Agrippa	3—M
Vast numbers in siege of Jerusalem, why	3—U
Various dates for ascension of Menes	5—H
Vision of the cross, famous	7—T
Worship of animals by Egyptians	2—P
Walls and gates of ancient Babylon	2—Q
Wicked, dying designs of Herod	3—J
Wesley and Methodism	4—I
Weddas, or evolution turned around	5—G
Willows and rivers of Babylon	6—L
Wine and bread for communion	6—Z
West and East, Empire divided into	8—J
Western and Eastern churches	8—K
Xerxes I riches; rouses nation against Greece	10—J
Xerxes I last Persian ruler of any note	10—K
Zuingli and the "Reformed Church"	4—D

SCRIPTURE INDEX

Following is a list of references through the Bible where the historical quotations may be applied:

Gen.	3:15	2—H		Josh.	3:15	6—G
	5:2	2—G		Neh.	8:8	6—D
	10:21	1—D		Psa.	90:9	10—B
	17:25	2—J			137:2	6—L
	19:14	2—N				
	30:3	6—K		Isa.	1:29	5—R
	31:19	1—A			2:18-21	5—R
	31:20	6—J			10:13	3—A
	35:2	1—A			13:1	1—W
	46:34	2—K			13:19-22	2—Y
					14:22, 23	2—Y
Ex.	1:15	2—I			17:8	5—R
	1:16	6—K			18:2	5—X
	8:26	2—P			19:4	5—T
	29:29, 30	2—O			19:18	1—J
	32:4	2—P			19:18	1—K
					19:19	1—M
Num.	28:3-6	1—G			19:22-25	5—U
	31:16	3—F			20:4	5—V
	34:5	2—E			21:2	1—W
					21:9	1—W
Deut.	11:10, 11	5—W			25:2	2—Y
	25:3	6—V			27:9	5—R
	26:5	6—J			30:22	5—R
	28:68	3—W			31:7	5—R
					41:11, 12	2—Y

	42:17	5—R	Jer.	50:13	2—Y
	43:17	2—Y		50:20	5—R
	45:1	2—Q		50:39, 40	2—Y
	45:1	8—G		50:44	6—D
	46:1, 2	1—W		51:26, 36	2—Y
	46:1, 2	2—Y		51:31, 32	8—G
	47:1-5	1—W			
	47:1-5	2—Y	Lam.	1:21, 22	2—Y
	48:14	2—Y			
	51:22, 23	2—Y	Ezk.	11:18	5—R
	59:18-21	2—Y		16:61	5—R
				20:38, 43	5—R
Jer.	1:13, 14	5—S		26:7	3—C
	3:12	5—S		26:7	5—S
	3:24, 25	5—R		29:1, 12	3—B
	4:6	5—S		29:18	3—C
	4:7	6—G		30:24	3—B
	4:19	6—H		32:11	3—B
	6:1	5—S		36:25, 31	5—R
	9:17	3—R		37:23	5—R
	10:22	5—S		39:7	5—R
	12:5	6—G		43:10	5—R
	13:20	5—S			
	16:15	5—S	Dan.	2:39	2—D
	23:8	5—S		2:40	2—C
	23:20	5—R		5:1, 7, 16	5—O
	25:12-14	1—W		5:18, 22	8—A
	30:16, 23	2—Y		5:31	6—M
	33:8	5—R		7:5	1—V
	43:8-13	3—B		7:6	2—A
	46:2, 10	3—B		7:7	2—C
	46:13, 26	3—B		8:3	1—V
	46:20	5—S		8:5	1—Y
	49:19	6—G		8:7	1—X
	49:34-38	1—X		8:8	7—U
	49:34	1—Y		8:8	2—A

Dan.	8:9	2—R			24:16	9—I
	8:9	9—N			24:20	8—Y
	8:22	1—Z			24:21	2—W
	8:25	2—S			24:21	3—O
	9:1	6—M			24:28	2—U
	10:1	6—M				
	11:1	6—M		Mark	11:13	2—V
	11:4	2—A			13:14	2—T
	11:8	5—U				
	11:11	2—R		Luke	2:3, 5	9—R
	11:31	2—R			13:33	1—Q
	11:31	9—N			17:37	2—U
					19:44	2—X
Hos.	2:17	5—R			21:18	2—T
	14:8	5—R				
				John	9:2	6—W
Amos	1:1	9—L				
				Acts	1:12	8—Y
Mic.	5:13	5—R			12:21-23	3—M
					17:21	6—A
Nah.	2:10	3—A			23:5	5—Q
	3:7	3—A				
	3:17-19	3—A		1 Cor.	7:18	1—L
Zeph.	2:13-15	3—A		2 Cor.	11:24	6—V
Zech.	9:3	3—D		Phil.	2:1	6—H
	14:5	9—L				
				Col.	3:12	6—H
Matt.	1:20	2—N				
	2:1	2—P		2 Th.	2:7	4—X
	2:1	6—X				
	21:19	2—V		Jas.	4:14	10—B
	23:15	6—T				
	24:10	2—X		1 Jno.	3:17	6—H
	24:16	2—T				
				Rev.	12:6	9—Z

Additional references in 11th chapter of Daniel:

Vs. 2	10—J	Vs. 14	10—V	Vs. 29, 30	11—E
3, 4	10—K	18	10—W	30-35	11—F
4	10—L	19	10—X	32, 34	11—G
6	10—M	20	10—Y	36	11—H
7-9	10—N	21	10—Z	37	11—I
8	10—O	21	11—I	38, 39	11—F
10	10—P	22	11—A	38, 39	11—H
11	10—Q	23	11—B	40, 43	11—C
12	10—R	24-26	11—C	44, 45	11—J
13	10—S	27	11—D		
14	10—T	28	11—F		

This book is part of the *Ancient Landmarks Collection*.

Those in previous generations of what we often call the Restoration Movement produced a wealth of material that is useful for us today – either for instruction or as a matter of historical perspective or both. Many of these materials are rare and difficult to find. In order to make some of these materials accessible to this generation, Gospel Armory is working to republish some of the works by men of the past.

Other titles in the collection include:

> *Biographies of Restoration Pioneers (Volume 2)* by Kyle D. Frank – This book contains twenty-one biographical sketches of preachers associated with the Restoration Movement. They are presented in a concise, easy-to-read format. All who are interested in learning from the past will benefit from the material in this volume.
>
> *The Gospel Preacher: Volume 2* by Benjamin Franklin – This book contains twenty-one sermons Franklin, one of the most influential preachers among conservative brethren in the nineteenth century.

For a complete list of titles currently available, visit www.gospelarmory.com/ancient-landmarks-collection

Made in the USA
Columbia, SC
04 January 2024